Crawford Howell Toy

The History of the Religion of Israel

an Old Testament primer. Third Edition

Crawford Howell Toy

The History of the Religion of Israel
an Old Testament primer. Third Edition

ISBN/EAN: 9783337092276

Printed in Europe, USA, Canada, Australia, Japan

Cover: Foto ©Andreas Hilbeck / pixelio.de

More available books at **www.hansebooks.com**

THE HISTORY

OF

THE RELIGION OF ISRAEL:

An Old Testament Primer.

BY

CRAWFORD H. TOY,

PROFESSOR OF HEBREW LANGUAGE AND LITERATURE IN
HARVARD UNIVERSITY.

THIRD EDITION.

BOSTON:
UNITARIAN SUNDAY-SCHOOL SOCIETY,
7 TREMONT PLACE.
1884.

UNIVERSITY PRESS:
JOHN WILSON AND SON, CAMBRIDGE.

PREFACE.

It has been thought best to present the whole History of Israel in one course of lessons. This could not be done without great compression of the matter; but it is hoped that the Primer in this shape will not be beyond the grasp of children of twelve years and upwards.

Where the condensation is so great, much is necessarily left to the knowledge and discretion of the teacher. He must treat the various subjects as he thinks best for his class, — abridging here, and expanding there; dividing one lesson into two, or throwing two into one; omitting one or more lessons, if he thinks fit, and substituting for them other matter. He must freely discuss the opinions expressed in the Primer, dissenting from and modifying them according to his best judgment.

One or two suggestions may be made as to the conduct of the lessons. It is very desirable that the teacher should bring himself into hearty sympathy with the period studied, so as to give his pupils a vivid picture of its outward circumstances and its thought. The cultivation of the historical sense will be worth more than the acquisition of facts. To aid him in this task a short list of books of reference is appended to each lesson. Only such books are mentioned as it is believed will be useful to Sunday-school instructors. Every Sunday-school should have a reference library. (See the List of Books on page xi; also Catalogue of Books recommended by the Ladies' Commission, Boston, 1871.)

Maps and charts should be freely used. Each class ought to have its own apparatus of these necessary helps to historical study.

Words strange to children should be carefully explained. Occasionally it may be well to spend the whole time of the lesson in fixing in the pupil's mind the signification of a single term; for example, "monotheism." When he has once really acquired this, it will save him from many misconceptions, and make all his succeeding reading easier.

The scholars must be encouraged to read the Old Testament, not as a lesson, but for its own sake; and each one should be provided with, and should bring regularly to the class, a copy of the Bible. The Apocrypha, also, should be accessible. The teacher may suggest a chapter in one of the historical books, or the prophets, or elsewhere, and try to awaken a lively interest in it. If possible, he should talk with the scholars on such passages outside of the school-room.

It is suggested that the Introductory Lesson be gone over rapidly at the beginning of the course, and then more carefully at its close. But this, as well as quarterly and other reviews, must be left to the teacher's judgment, or the decision of the school. The writer of these lessons, feeling strongly their meagreness, will be very glad to give such aid as he can to those teachers who may think it worth their while to apply to him.

OCTOBER, 1882.

NOTE. — The third issue is substantially identical with the first and second, differing from them only in a few statements of detail.

OCTOBER, 1884.

CONTENTS.

	PAGE
PREFACE	iii
CHRONOLOGICAL TABLE	ix
BOOKS OF REFERENCE	xi
INTRODUCTORY LESSON	1

LESSON I. — The Beginnings of Hebrew History. The Races of the Earth. The Migrations of the Semites. The Nomadic Life of the Hebrews in Canaan. The Earliest Form of the Religion of Israel in Canaan. Their Worship. Their Language 9

LESSON II. — The Israelites in Egypt. The Greatness of the Egyptians. The Fertility of Egypt — Dependence of the Desert Tribes on it. The Israelites in Goshen. How the Israelites lived in Goshen. The Israelites forced into Hard Labor by the Egyptians 13

LESSON III. — The Exodus and Moses. Bible Account of Moses and the Exodus. The Exodus and the March to Canaan. The Traditional Account of the Origin of the Law of Israel. What the Early Prophets said of Moses — Whether he borrowed anything from the Egyptians. Israelitish Customs before Moses 18

LESSON IV. — Moses and Yahwe (Jehovah). Yahwe, the God of Israel — His Original Character. Whether Moses Introduced the Worship of Yahwe — Whether he was a Monotheist. Is the Decalogue Monotheistic? Moses' Work Uncertain. What Moses probably did 23

LESSON V. — The Conquest and the Judges. The March from Goshen to Canaan. The Book of Joshua. The Time of the Judges. The Book of Judges. The Principal Judges. Civil and Religious Character of this Period . . 27

LESSON VI. — Samuel and Saul. The Situation in the Time of Eli. Samuel's Life and Work. The Life of Saul. The First Book of Samuel 32

LESSON VII. — David and Solomon. Legends of Great Men. David as King and Man. David as Religious Man and Poet. Solomon as King and Sage. Solomon's Temple. The Books of Kings and Chronicles. The Chronology . . 36

LESSON VIII. — Worship of the Calf and of Baal. The Division of the Kingdom. The Dynasties of Jeroboam and Omri. Calf-Worship and Baal-Worship. Elijah and Elisha. Political and Religious History of Judah 42

LESSON IX. — The Fall of the Baal-Worship. The Contrast between the Worships of Israel and Canaan. Elijah and Elisha determine to root out Baalism. Jehu's Reform. The Dynasty of Jehu. Political History of Judah. Religion in Judah 47

LESSON X. — The Prophets Amos and Hosea. Development of Israelitish Literature. The Different Sorts of Prophets and their Writings. Amos. Hosea. The Influence of Amos and Hosea 51

LESSON XI. — The Fall of Israel. Ahaz and Hezekiah in Judah. The Fall of the Northern Kingdom. The Fate of the Israelites. Political History of Judah under Ahaz and Hezekiah. Religious History of Judah 56

LESSON XII. — The Prophets Micah and Isaiah. The Groups of Prophets. The Times of Micah and Isaiah. Micah. The Life of Isaiah. Isaiah's Prophecies. Isaiah's Hope of the Future 60

CONTENTS. vii

PAGE

LESSON XIII. — The Reform of Josiah. Partial Character of Hezekiah's Reform. The Reaction under Manasseh. Progress of the Yahwe Party. The Book of Deuteronomy. Reform under Josiah 65

LESSON XIV. — Jeremiah and the Fall of Jerusalem. The Capture of Jerusalem by the Chaldeans. Nahum, Zephaniah, and Habakkuk. Jeremiah's Life. His Faith and Teaching. His Book 69

LESSON XV. — The Exile. The Carrying Away of the Jews to Babylon. The Results of the Exile. Historical Books written at this Time. Obadiah and Lamentations 74

LESSON XVI. — The Prophets of the Exile. Condition of the Exiles. Ezekiel. The Second Isaiah. Other Exilian Writings 79

LESSON XVII. — History and Prophetic Writings up to the Time of the Maccabees. Character of the Period. The Return from Exile. The Building of the Temple. Haggai and Zechariah. The History up to the Maccabees. Joel, Zechariah II., Zechariah III., Malachi 83

LESSON XVIII. — Ezra's Reform, and the Pentateuch. Progress of Legal and Priestly Ideas. What Ezra did. Formation of the Pentateuch. Character of the Pentateuch 89

LESSON XIX. — Literature of the Ezra Period. The Period of Ezra. The Book of Chronicles. The Books of Ezra and Nehemiah. The Book of Jonah. The Book of Esther. The Book of Job 93

LESSON XX. — The Hasmoneans. The Struggle for Freedom. Antiochus Epiphanes. The Two Jewish Parties. The War of Freedom. The Hasmonean Dynasty. The Three Sects or Parties 99

LESSON XXI. — Later Literature. 1. Ritual and Didactic. The Classes of the Literature. Psalms. Proverbs. Ecclesiasticus; or, the Wisdom of the Son of Sirach. The Wisdom of Solomon. Ecclesiastes; or, the Preacher. The Song of Songs 103

LESSON XXII. Later Literature. 2. Apocalyptic. 3. Philosophical and Historical. Character of the Apocalyptic Literature. Daniel. The Sibyl. Enoch. Ezra. Other Works 108

LESSON XXIII. — The Canon. Definition of "Canon." The Time before Ezra. The Pentateuch. The Prophetical Books. The Hagiographa. The Alexandrian Canon. The Samaritan Canon 113

LESSON XXIV. — The Scribes. The Study of the Law. Formation of the Class of Scribes. Schools and Teachers. The Sanhedrin. Method and Influence of the Scribes . . 118

LESSON XXV. — The Fall of Jerusalem. The Herod Family. The Roman Procurators. The Uprising and Fall. Change of Language. Christianity 123

LESSON XXVI. — The Talmud. The Later Judaism. The Mishna. The Gemara. Contents of the Talmud. Other Literature 128

LESSON XXVII. — The Remaining Literature. Philo and Josephus. Bible Translations. The Masora. Grammars and Dictionaries. Expository and Philosophical Works. Cabbala. The Karaites. Poetry 132

LESSON XXVIII. — Outward History from the Fall of Jerusalem. Proselyting. History in Palestine. In Babylonia. In Europe. Messianic Expectations 138

LESSON XXIX. — The Reform. Intellectual Isolation of the Jews. Progress. Moses Mendelssohn. Progress since Mendelssohn. The Present Condition of the Reform. The Orthodox 143

LESSON XXX. — Conclusion. The Persistence of the Religion of Israel. Its Character and Growth. Its Legacy to us 147

CHRONOLOGICAL TABLE.

B.C.	HISTORY.	LITERATURE.
2000.	Migration of Hebrews from Mesopotamia.	Egyptian Book of the Dead.
1800.	First abode of the Hebrews in Egypt.	
1600.	Settlement of the Israelites in Egypt.	
1330.	Exodus under Moses.	
1300.	Conquest of Canaan by the Israelites.	Folk-poetry in Israel.
1080.	Samuel.	
1060.	Accession of Saul.	
1040.	Accession of David.	Beginning of written records in Israel. Lyrical pieces.
1000.	Accession of Solomon.	Beginning of Israelitish gnomic literature.
960.	Division of the kingdom. Accession of Jeroboam of Israel and Rehoboam of Judah.	First attempts at connected historical writing.
942.	Accession of Asa of Judah.	
915.	Accession of Omri of Israel.	
903.	Accession of Ahab of Israel.	
901.	Accession of Jehoshaphat of Judah.	
900.	Elijah begins his prophetic work.	
842.	Overthrow of the Omri dynasty by Jehu. Prophet Elisha active. Athaliah usurps the throne of Judah.	First written collections of laws.
785.	Accession of Jeroboam II. of Israel.	Prophets Amos and Hosea.
726.	Accession of Hezekiah of Judah.	Prophets Isaiah and Micah.
720.	Fall of the kingdom of Israel.	
697.	Accession of Manasseh.	Various lyrical religious pieces.
650.		Prophet Nahum.
639.	Accession of Josiah.	
623.		Deuteronomy, Zephaniah.
609.	Battle of Megiddo and death of Josiah.	
606.		Habakkuk.
597.	Deportation of Jews to Babylon.	Jeremiah. 626–580. Ezekiel. 593–570.
586.	Fall of the kingdom of Judah.	
580.		Obadiah. Lamentations. Psalms.
560.		Judges, Ruth, Samuel, and Kings.
540.		The Second Isaiah.
539.	Capture of Babylon by Cyrus.	
536.	Return of the Jews to Canaan.	
521.		Haggai, Zech. i.–viii.
515.	Completion of the second temple.	
457.	First visit of Ezra to Jerusalem.	

CHRONOLOGICAL TABLE.

B.C.	HISTORY.	LITERATURE.
444.	Nehemiah governor of Judea. Ezra and Nehemiah introduce the nearly completed Law.	
420.		Malachi.
400.		The Pentateuch receives its final form.
300.		Chronicles, Zech. ix.-xiv., Joel.
275.		Septuagint begun.
195.	Onias III. high-priest.	Esther.
170.	Antiochus Epiphanes profanes the temple of Jerusalem.	
167.	Revolt of the Jews.	
164.	Judas Maccabæus purifies the temple. Institution of the Feast of Dedication.	Daniel.
150.		Psalms and Proverbs completed.
130.	John Hyrcanus I. destroys the Samaritan temple on Mt. Gerizim.	Eccles. Song of Songs. Son of Sirach. Ecclus. I. Maccabees.
100.		Close of the Canon. Septuagint [completed.
63.	Pompey takes Jerusalem.	
40.	Herod king of Judea.	Book of Enoch.
17.	Begins to rebuild the temple.	
4.	Birth of Christ.	
A.D		
70.	Destruction of Jerusalem.	
132.	Messianic uprising under Bar-cochba.	
150.		Targum of Onkelos. Greek version of Old Testament by Aquila.
192.		The Mishna.
250.		Targum of Jonathan.
350.		Jerusalem Talmud.
490.		Babylonian Talmud.
1036.	Overthrow of the Babylonian Patriarchate.	
1204.	Death of Maimonides.	
1492.	Expulsion of the Jews from Spain.	
1518.		Bomberg's Rabbinical Bible.
1575.	Death of Joseph Karo, the second Maimonides.	
1666.	The pretended Messiah, Shabbathai Zwi. sets out on his march to Jerusalem.	
1786.	Death of Moses Mendelssohn.	

BOOKS OF REFERENCE.

NOTE. — For the convenience of Bible-teachers, the following list of books of reference on the Old Testament, fuller than those given in the text, is appended. In imported books the shilling represents about 35 cents, the mark about the same, and the franc about 30 cents. By direct importation through the mail, these prices may be lowered.

☞ The most useful of the larger books for Sunday-School teachers are marked with one asterisk, and of these the most essential with two asterisks.

DICTIONARIES.

Smith's Dictionary of the Bible. American edition, by Hackett and Abbot. New York: Hurd & Houghton, 1868. 4 vols. $20.00.
—— Concise Dictionary. Boston. 1865. $4.50. *
—— Smaller Dictionary. Boston. 1865. $3.00.
Herzog's Real-Encyclopädie für Protestantische Theologie und Kirche. Leipzig: Hinrichs. New edition coming out by numbers, of which 105 have appeared. Per number, 1 mark.
Schenkel's Bibel-Lexicon. Leipzig: Brockhaus, 1865–75. 5 vols. 45 marks.
McClintock and Strong's Theological and Ecclesiastical Cyclopedia. New York: Harper and Brothers, 1869–. 10 vols. Per vol., 5.00. *
Kitto's Cyclopedia of Biblical Literature. Third edition. Philadelphia: Lippincott, 1870. $25.00.
—— Popular Cyclopedia. Philadelphia: Henry Bill, 1869. $4.50.
F. Lichtenberger, Encyclopédie des Sciences Religieuses. Paris: Fischbacher. 13 vols. Per vol., 12½ francs.
Cruden's Concordance, condensed. New York. $1.50. * *
R. D. Hitchcock, Analysis of the Bible (by subjects); with Cruden's Concordance as revised by Eadie. New York: A. J. Johnson, 1870. $6.00. *

CRITICISM.

F. Bleek, Introduction. English Translation. London: George Bell & Sons, 1875. 2 vols. 10 shillings. *

—— Einleitung. Edited by J. Wellhausen. Berlin: G. Reimer, 1878. 10½ marks.

W. M. L. De Wette, Einleitung. Edited by E. Schrader. Berlin: G. Reimer, 1869. 8 marks.

J. W. Colenso, The Pentateuch and the Book of Joshua. London: Longmans, 1879. 5 vols. £2 10s.

—— The same, Popular Edition. $2.40.

—— The Pentateuch and the Moabite Stone. 1873. 12 shillings.

M. Heilprin, Historical Poetry of the Ancient Hebrews. New York: Appleton, 1879-80. 2 vols. $2.00.

T. C. Murray, Origin of the Psalms. New York: Scribner, 1880. $1.50. *

S. Davidson, Introduction. London: Williams & Norgate, 1862-63. 3 vols. $4.20.

I. Taylor, The Spirit of Hebrew Poetry. N. Y. 1863. $1.50. *

J. G. Palfrey, Lectures on the Jewish Scriptures and Antiquities. Boston. 1838-52. 4 vols. $15.00. Out of print.

COMMENTARIES.

Bunsen's Bibel-Werk. Leipzig: Brockhaus, 1858-70. About $20.00.

Philippson's Israelitische Bibel (Hebrew and German, with notes). Leipzig: Baumgärtner, 1888. About $25.00.

Lange's Commentary on the Old Testament. American Translation. New York: Scribner, 1869-80. 15 vols. $5.00 per vol. The volumes on Kings, Jeremiah, Ezekiel, Daniel, and the Apocrypha may be especially commended.

Edouard Reuss. La Bible. Paris: Fischbacher, 1874-81. 19 vols. 170 francs. *

The Annotated Paragraph Bible. London: Religious Tract Society, 1867. The Notes are short and clear. American Reprint, about $7.00. * *

The Bible Commentary (sometimes called The Speaker's Commentary). New York: Scribner, 1871-75. 6 vols. $5.00 per vol. See especially the notes on Chronicles, Jeremiah, Ezekiel, Daniel, and the Minor Prophets.

Kurzgefasstes Exegetisches Handbuch. Leipzig: S. Hirzel. About 8 marks per vol. The various volumes are, from time to time, re edited or rewritten. Among the best are those on Genesis, Exodus, Leviticus, Job (Dillmann), Psalms (Olshausen), Ezekiel (Smend), Minor Prophets (Steiner). *

On Genesis. M. M. Kalisch. London: Longmans & Co. Hebrew and English. 1858. 18 shillings. Abridged edition, 12 shillings.

On Exodus. The same. Hebrew and English. 1855. 15 shillings. Abridged edition, 12 shillings.

On Leviticus. The same. Hebrew and English. 1867-72. 30 shillings. Abridged edition, 16 shillings.

On the Prophets. H. Ewald. English Translation. London: Williams & Norgate, 1875-81. 5 vols. About $31.75. *

—— G. R. Noyes. Boston: American Unitarian Association, 1874. 2 vols. $1.25 per vol. *

On Isaiah. T. K. Cheyne. 2 vols. London: C. Kegan Paul & Co., 1880-82. 25 shillings. *

—— Fr. Delitzsch. New York: Scribner. 2 vols. $3.00 per vol.

On Ezekiel. Patrick Fairbairn. New York: Scribner. $5.00.

On the Minor Prophets. E. Henderson. Andover: W. F. Draper, 1868. $4.00.

On Haggai, Zechariah, and Malachi. M. Pressel. Gotha: Schloesmann, 1870. 7 marks. *

On Zechariah. C. H. H. Wright (Bampton Lectures for 1878). New York: E. P. Dutton & Co. About $1.25.

On the Psalms. J. J. S. Perowne. Andover: W. F. Draper, 1870. 2 vols. $6.75.

—— Fr. Delitzsch. English Translation. Edinburgh: T. and T. Clark, 1871. 3 vols. $3.00 per vol. *

—— A. Tholuck. English Translation. Philadelphia: W. S. & Alfred Martien, 1858. $2.25.

—— Charles Spurgeon. New York: Scribner. 4 vols. $4.00 per vol.

—— H. Ewald. English Translation. London: Williams and Norgate, 1880-81. 2 vols. $2.75 per vol. *

—— A. Barnes. New York: Harper & Brothers, 1876. 3 vols. $1.50 per vol.

—— and the Proverbs: G. R. Noyes. Boston: American Unitarian Association. $1.25. *

On the Proverbs. F. Delitzsch. English Translation. Edinburgh: T. & T. Clark, 1874. 2 vols. $3.00 per vol. *

On Job. Adalbert Merx. Jena: Dufft, 1871. 6 marks.
—— E. Renan. Paris: Lévy, 1865. 7½ francs.
—— F. Delitzsch. 1869. 2 vols. $3.00 per vol. *
—— A. Barnes. New York: Leavitt & Allen, 1867. 2 vols. About $1.75 per vol.
—— J. A. Froude, Short Studies. I.
—— Ecclesiastes and the Canticles. G. R. Noyes. Boston American Unitarian Association. $1.25. *
On the Song of Songs. H. Graetz. Vienna: Braumüller, 1871. 4 marks.
—— E. Renan. Paris: Lévy, 1860. 6 francs.
—— C. D. Ginsburg. London, 1867.
On Ecclesiastes. E. Renan. Paris: Calmann Lévy, 1882. 5 francs.
—— C. D. Ginsburg. London, 1861.
—— H. Graetz. Leipzig: Winter, 1871. 5¼ marks.
The Apocrypha (with marginal notes and references). London: Eyre & Spottiswoode. $1.50. * *
—— (without notes and references). London: Society for Promoting Christian Knowledge. 60 cents.
The Holy Scriptures of the Old Covenant. Revised Translation, by C. Wellbeloved, G. V. Smith, J. S. Porter. London: 1859-62. 3 vols. $6.75.
Variorum Bible. London: Eyre & Spottiswoode, 1880. $4.60 to $9.25, according to style. * *

HISTORY.

C. K. J. Bunsen, God in History. English Translation. London: Longman, Green, & Co., 1868. 3 vols. 42 shillings.
M. Duncker, History of Antiquity. English Translation. London: Bentley & Son, 1877-80. 4 vols. 21 shillings. * *
G. Maspero, Histoire Ancienne. Paris: Hachette & Cie., 1875. 5 francs.
L. Ménard, Hist. des Anciens Peuples de l'Orient. 1882. 4 francs.
Heinrich Brugsch, History of Egypt. English Translation. London: John Murray, 1879. 2 vols. 30 shillings.
G. Wilkinson, Manners and Customs of the Ancient Egyptians. New edition. London: John Murray, 1878. 3 vols. About 40 shillings.
G. Rawlinson, History of Egypt. New York: Dodd & Mead, 1881. 2 vols. $6.00. To be read with caution, especially the chronology and account of religion.
—— Ancient Monarchies. N. Y.: Dodd & Mead, 1881. 3 vols. $9.00.

Records of the Past (odd vols., Assyrian, even vols., Egyptian texts). London: Bagster. Begun in 1873, published from time to time. Per vol., 3s. 6d.

George Smith, Chaldean Genesis. Edited by A. H. Sayce. London: Low, 1881. 18 shillings.

—— Assyrian Canon. London: Bagster, 1875. 9 shillings.

C. P. Tiele: Outlines of the History of Religion. Boston: Houghton, Mifflin, & Co. $2.50.

—— Histoire Comparée des Anciennes Religions de l'Egypte et des Peuples Sémitiques. French Translation. Paris: G. Fischbacher, 1882. 12 francs. The best book on the subject.

—— Egyptian Religion. English Translation (English and Foreign Phil. Library). Boston: Houghton, Mifflin, & Co., 1882. $1.75. *

—— Assyrian Religion. English Translation. *

Hibbert Lectures. P. Le Page Renouf, Religion of Ancient Egypt. London: Williams & Norgate, 1880. 10s. 6d.

—— A. Kuenen. National Religions and Universal Religions. London, 1882. *

A. Kuenen, Religion of Israel. English Translation. London: Williams & Norgate, 1874. 3 vols. $9.00.

J. Wellhausen, Geschichte Israels. Berlin: G. Reimer. Vol. I., 1883. 6 marks.

H. Graetz, Geschichte der Juden (from the earliest times till the present day). Leipzig: O. Liner. Coming out in parts, at 20 cents each.

H. Ewald, History of Israel. English Translation. 5 vols. About $20.00.

E. H. Palmer, History of the Jewish Nation. London, 1874. About $2.25. *

A. Edersheim, Sketch of the Jewish Social Life in the Days of Christ. London: Religious Tract Society, 1876. $2.50. *

Oort and Hooykaas, Bible for Learners. English Translation. Boston: Roberts Brothers, 1878-81. 2 vols. (Old Test.) $4.00. * *

J. Knappert, Religion of Israel. English Translation. Boston: Roberts Brothers, 1878. $1.00. *

H. H. Milman, History of the Jews. New York: Widdleton. 3 vols. $1.50 per vol.

A. P. Stanley, Jewish Church. New York: Charles Scribner & Sons, 1870. 3 vols. $2.50 per vol. *

W. R. Smith, Old Testament in the Jewish Church. New York, D. Appleton & Co., 1881. $1.75. *

—— Prophets of Israel. New York: D. Appleton & Co., 1882. $1.75. *

BOOKS OF REFERENCE.

J. H. Allen, Hebrew Men and Times. Boston: Roberts Brothers, 1879. $1.50.

F. H. Hedge, Primeval World of Hebrew Tradition. Boston: Roberts Brothers, 1872. $1.50.

R. P. Smith, Prophecy a Preparation for Christ. London & New York: McMillan, 1871. $1.75.

A. Kuenen, Prophets and Prophecy in Israel. English Translation. London: Longmans, Green, & Co, 1877. 21 shillings.

B. Duhm, Theologie der Propheten. Bonn: Adolph Marcus, 1875. 6 marks.

F. D. Maurice, Prophets and Kings of the Old Testament. Boston: Crosby, Nichols, & Co., 1853. About $3.50.

J. Fürst, Der Canon des Alten Testaments. Leipzig: Dörffling & Franke, 1868. 2.40 marks.

S. Davidson, The Canon of the Bible. London: Henry S. King & Co., 1877. $2.50. *

Humphrey Prideaux, Connection of the Old and New Testaments. New York: Harper & Brothers, 1845. 2 vols. About $4.00. * *

Flavius Josephus, Complete Works. Translated by Whiston. Various editions, from $1.00 to $6.00. *

M. J. Raphall, Post-Biblical History of the Jews. Philadelphia; 1855. 2 vols. $3.00. Out of Print.

J. M. Jost, Geschichte des Judenthums und Seiner Secten. Leipzig: Dörffling & Franke, 1857-59. About 20 marks.

L. Wogue, Histoire de la Bible et de l'Exégèse Biblique. Paris: Imprimerie Nationale, 1881. 12 francs.

J. W. Etheridge, Introduction to Jewish Literature. London: Longman, Brown, Green, & Longman, 1856. About $3.00. *

J. Picciotto, Sketches of Anglo-Jewish History. London: Trübner & Co., 1875.

F. D. Mocatta, The Jews of Spain and Portugal, and the Inquisition. London, 1877. About $3.00.

A. Geiger, Judaism and its History. English Translation. New York: M. Thalmessing & Co. About $1.00.

M. A. Weill, Le Judaisme, ses Dogmas et sa Mission. Paris: Librairie Israëlite, 1866. 3 vols. 21 francs.

Charles Taylor, Sayings of the Jewish Fathers (translation of Talmud Tracts). Cambridge, England: University Press, 1877. About $3.00. *

F. Huidekoper, Judaism at Rome, B.C. 76–A.D 140. New York: James Miller. $2.25. *

J. T. Sunderland, What is the Bible? New York: G. P. Putnam's Sons, 1878. $1.00.

S. R. Calthrop, The Old Testament. Unitarian Review, October, 1880.

E. H. Hall, The Bible. Unitarian Review, October, 1880; also in Ninth Report of National Unitarian Conference, 1881.

Institute Essays. Boston: G. H. Ellis, 1880. $1.25.

J. W. Chadwick, The Bible of To-day. New York: G. P. Putnam's Sons. $1.75.

W. C. Gannett, A Chosen Nation; or, The Growth of the Hebrew Religion. Chicago: Western Unitarian Sunday-School Society. 15 cents. Chart to accompany the same, 5 cents.

R. P. Stebbins, A Study of the Pentateuch. Boston: George H. Ellis, 1882. $1.25.

GEOGRAPHY AND ARCHÆOLOGY.

Edward Robinson, Biblical Researches in Palestine. Boston: Crocker & Brewster, 1856-57. 3 vols. with maps, 1 vol. $10.00.

A. P. Stanley, Sinai and Palestine. New York: Widdleton. $2.50.

Jahn's Archæology. English Translation. N. Y. 1853. $2.00. *

S. Clark, Bible Atlas, with index of Names. London: Society for Promoting Christian Knowledge, 1868. $7.50. * *

E. P. Barrows, Sacred Geography and Antiquities. New York: American Tract Society. $2.25. * *

Collins's Atlas of Scripture Geography. Glasgow: William Collins, Sons, & Co. 16 maps. 9 pence.

James Fergusson, Temples of the Jews. London: John Murray, 1878.

H. B. Tristram, Natural History of the Bible. London. 1867. About $3.00. *

J. G. Wood, Bible Animals. New York. 1870. $5.00. *

HISTORY

OF

THE RELIGION OF ISRAEL.

HISTORY

OF

THE RELIGION OF ISRAEL.

INTRODUCTORY LESSON.

BEFORE beginning our study of the history of the Israelitish religion, it may be well to take a general survey of the course of its development, in order to fix in our minds its main epochs and its salient facts. At the same time the general plan of the following lessons will thus be brought out.

§ 1. THE DIVISIONS OF THE HISTORY.

Divisions. — We give these lessons the title "History of the Religion of Israel," because there is little to study in Israel beside its religion (no art, science, philosophy, to speak of), and because we wish to trace its historical development. We make five divisions: 1. The *formative*, extending from the earliest times to about the end of the ninth century B.C.; 2. The *prophetic*, from this point to the Exile, sixth century B.C., the Exile being a transition period; 3. The *priestly*, from the return to about the first century B.C.; 4. The *scribal*, extending from this point on to the eighteenth century of our era; 5. The *modern*, including the last hundred years. It will be understood that these division-marks are to be taken in a general way; the different periods overlap and melt into one another.

1. Progress in the First Period. — During the first period things are in an unsettled condition. The wandering, half-civilized Israelitish tribes gradually draw closer together, come into permanent habitations, and are compacted into a firm kingly government (eleventh century B.C.), though they immediately afterwards split into two kingdoms, each of which goes its own way. At the same time the religion becomes more defined in its outward form and its inward meaning. The people cast away a number of their ancient deities, and practically restrict themselves, so far as their own circle of divinities is concerned, to their national god, Yahwe. They were, however, at this time by no means monotheists. They regarded the gods of other nations as real beings, and they adopted the worships of their Canaanite neighbors. But Yahwe was the god of Israel alone, and they clung to him. Their ethical notions and practices were rude, — there was much violence and cruelty; but more enlightened ideas gradually established themselves, till, towards the end of this first period, the social life was tolerably firm and kindly. Temples were built, and a regular priesthood and religious service instituted. A beginning was made in literature: short poems and sketches of history and tradition were written.

2. Second Period. — The second period is perhaps the most remarkable in Jewish history. It was not outwardly successful, for during its progress the two Israelitish kingdoms were destroyed, and the people carried off, some to Assyria, some to Babylon. But the religion made a great stride forward. The prophets insisted that Yahwe alone, to the exclusion of all other gods, was to be worshipped by Israel: and at last they preached that there was no other god but Yahwe, and that he should be worshipped not only by Israel, but by all nations. This was true monotheism, and the Jews have taught it to us and to all the world. This is their contribution to the world's stock of ideas. Some other details of religious life they may have worked out, but this is their glory.

In this second period, also, the Israelites began to regulate their temple-worship, define the duties and privileges of priests, and record their religious law in books (Deuteronomy, seventh century B.C.).

Their ethical conceptions grew in purity and definiteness. They dwelt more and more on the nobler attributes of God, his holiness and justice, his faithfulness and love. It is from the prophets mainly that we learn this.

3. Third Period. — The prophetic period was the fresh, creative youth of Israel. To this succeeds the time of reflection, when, the great principles of religion having been established and nothing more in that direction possible, there begins the desire to regulate the religious life by fixed precepts. Israel has sought the one God and found him, and now feels that its task is to maintain his service and secure his favor by following rules. This, then, is the legal period, which was controlled first by priests and then by scribes. The priests began to draw up ritual codes during the Exile (Ezekiel), and they continued this work till the present Law of the Pentateuch was completed (fifth century B.C.). The prophets after the Exile were few and weak. Israel had become the "people of the book." They were pure theists, but they began to give the most of their thought to the ceremonies of religion. During this period their political life flashed out into splendor for one brief moment under the Maccabees (second century B.C.), and then sank forever.

4. Fourth Period. Study of the Law and Tradition. — The scribes were the successors of the prophets and the priests, — of the former inasmuch as they were the expounders of principles of religion, and of the latter in so far as they were occupied with explaining the ritual law. We have seen what an important work the prophets accomplished. Priests also had existed, of course, from the beginning; there were always altars and sacrifices. The priestly period represents the natural devotion to the temple, as the visible centre and sign of religious life and of the presence of God, when the creative impulse of the prophets had died out. It might seem to us that God spoke more directly to Israel through the prophets; yet he led Israel no less surely by priests and scribes. The priests, during and after the Exile, were also scribes, that is, students and expounders of the law. And before the beginning of our era schools had been established for this legal study; at that time law and theology were one and the same. Priests and scribes stood side by side; the former conducted the public religious service, the latter explained its rules and principles. But after the destruction of the temple of Jerusalem by the Romans (A.D. 70) the priesthood vanished, — there was nothing more for it to do. From that time for seventeen hundred years the religious thought of the Jews consisted in study of the law, written and traditional. The written law is contained in the Pentateuch. But many of its prescriptions required explanation, and this was given orally by the teachers (rabbis). These explanations soon formed a large mass of traditions (they may be compared to our Common Law), and after a while were gathered up and committed to writing (Talmud); the Jews then became the people of the Talmud. This study was not lacking in results. It sharpened the intellect and it produced a great legal code. But it spent most of its force on little things; it was like the scholastic philosophy in its tendency to quibble, but it had no such future as that philosophy. It was devoid of religious life.

In the midst of this period Christ appeared and Christianity was established; but, though it sprang out of Judaism, which had prepared its way, it had no appreciable influence on Jewish thought. Israel remained separate in the world. Scattered over the face of the earth, the Jews entered into civil relations with Greeks and Romans, Persians, Mohammedans, and Christians; but their religion remained about the same that Christ found it.

5. Fifth Period. Reason in Religion. — Such was their position up to a hundred years ago. They were blind followers of authority; they would not believe that anything could be learned outside of the Scripture (the Old Testament) and the Talmud. But towards the close of the last century a body of Jewish thinkers, imbued with the German philosophy of that period, asserted the right to use the reason in the determination of religious belief and practice. They simplified the creed, reducing it to a confession of faith in God, and threw off the authority of the Talmud. They were followed by large numbers of Israelites in Europe and America, who constitute the body known as the Reform, while the Talmudists are called the Orthodox. The Reform Jews, who are now in the majority, have distinguished themselves by scientific research. They have no creed, but represent all phases of religious belief. And in fact it is not the historical faith of Israel that they profess. They are merely Jews who have reached modern (Christian) ideas of religion. It is the Orthodox, or Talmudists, who are the formal continuers of the religion of the old prophets and scribes, though the Reform has more of the old prophetic spirit.

QUESTIONS.

What is the title of this course of lessons? Why is it chosen? What are the divisions of the history?

1. In the first period, what progress was made in the organization of society? — in religion? — in morals? — in literature?

2. In the second period, what progress was made in the conception of God? — in the outward forms of religion? — in ethical ideas?

3. What is the legal period? Why is Israel called "the people of the book"? What brilliant political record in this period? — its date?

4. Of whom were the scribes the successors? When did the priests begin to study the Law? When did the priesthood vanish? Who were the rabbis? What is the Talmud? Were the Jews much affected by Christianity?

5. When did the Jews begin to be imbued with modern European philosophical and religious ideas? What is the difference between the Orthodox and the Reform Jews? Is the Jewish Reform really a Jewish religious movement?

§ 2. THE LITERATURE.

In the following lessons we shall speak of the literature along with the various periods of the history; but here we shall give a connected view of its development.

1. Writings of the Ninth Century B.C. — The first Israelitish writings that we can clearly trace appeared in the times of the early kings, probably about the ninth century B.C. Before that period poets had recited odes, and fathers had related to their children stories of the olden times and incidents of later years.

But now books began to be composed. There were poetical compilations, such as "The Book of the Wars of Yahwe" (Num. xxi. 14) and "The Book of Yashar" (Jashar, Josh. x. 13, 2 Sam. i. 18); prose histories of the kings, and perhaps of the patriarchs, forming the basis of our present historical books; and perhaps, also, some simple collections of laws, like that in Exodus xxi.–xxiii. These were all brief and occasional; there was nothing connected and extensive.

2. Writings from the Eighth Century to the Sixth B.C. Prophets and Historians. Law Books and Proverbs. — From the eighth century B.C. on, the Israelites show great increase of literary skill. They were advancing in civilization. With greater quiet, stability, wealth, and leisure, there grew up a class of men who devoted themselves to study and writing. They began to have wider relations with surrounding nations. Their thought became more connected and far-reaching. The prophets pronounced and wrote their eloquent discourses. Poets began to compose hymns for religious worship. A comparatively large law book was written (Deuteronomy, about B.C. 622); and this, in accordance with the ideas of the time, which demanded the authority of ancient sages and law-givers, was ascribed to Moses. There were collections of the sayings of wise men (Prov. xxv. 1, about B.C. 710). And then came more regular works of history: during the Exile were written our books of Judges, Samuel, and Kings, and probably Ruth. Historical writing marks the rise of the reflective period in a nation's history. But Israel's historical works were all religious; they were designed to exhibit God's guidance of the people; they were sermons made up of selections from history. There is no constructive art in them; they are merely collections of facts to point a religious moral. For this reason the Israelitish mode of writing history is called "pragmatic."

3. Legal Writings. The Canons of the Law and the Prophets. — Next naturally followed the legal literature. After various law books had been written they were all gathered up, sifted, and edited about the time of Ezra (B.C. 450) as one book.

This is substantially our present Law (*Tora*) or Pentateuch. It was then accepted as a sacred book. This was the beginning of the Jewish Canon, or collection of sacred books. After a while (perhaps about B.C. 400) the writings of the prophets and the earlier historical books (those composed during the Exile, and Joshua) were gathered into a second part of the Canon.

4. The Writings of the Sages, and the later Historical Books. The Third Canon. — The ancient Israelites never pursued philosophy, in our sense of the word. But in this later period of their history they discussed questions of life and religion, inquiring into the ways of God with man, and asking concerning the best principles of living. Of this species of literature we have the books of Job, Ecclesiastes, Wisdom of Solomon, and Wisdom of the Son of Sirach. To these we may add the book of Proverbs and some of the Psalms (such as xxxvii., xlix., lxxiii.). Here we have the answers that wise men of Israel gave to the deeper problems of life. It is no longer prophets pouring out passionate appeals for God, or priests telling of sacrifices, but sages wrestling with doubts and fears.

Other histories were written at this time: the object of Chronicles (fourth century B.C.) was to describe the history of Israel in its relation to the temple-service; and the books of Ezra and Nehemiah are continuations of this description. Then there were what may be called historical romances, such as Jonah, Esther, Tobit, and Judith. There was also the Song of Songs, a poem in honor of pure wedded love. Finally, in the days of the Maccabees (second century B.C.) were produced the apocalyptic book of Daniel and the history of the Maccabean struggle. None of these latest books show the religious freshness of the prophets; only in the poetry of the Psalms (which continued to be composed down to the second century B.C.) we find smoothness of form and depth of national religious feeling. Israel had lost its creative power of thought. About a hundred years before the beginning of our era these were gathered into a third part of the sacred Canon. All of them were accepted as sacred by the Egyptian Jews, but some of them were for various reasons rejected by the Jews of Palestine; these last are called apocryphal books (they may be found in some editions of the Bible).

5. The Rabbinical Writings. — A few other works were produced by the Jews during the second and first centuries before Christ, such as Ezekiel's tragedy on the Mosaic history, and the apocalyptic Sibylline Oracles and books of Enoch and the Jubilees. But the people now threw itself into the study of the legal traditions. In Alexandria the influence of Greek thought was felt to some extent (Philo, A.D. 50), but the body of the nation was little affected thereby. The Talmud occupied Israel for seventeen centuries. Learned men did little but write commentaries on the Bible or the tradition. Even what they did in the shape of grammars and dictionaries (which was, however, valuable) was to assist the study of the Scripture. There was little new thought; the most was cast in a Talmudical mould. They studied Aristotle and the Arabian writers, but it was for the sake of the Talmud. Here and there arose a great thinker who gave some impulse to his people's life; but as a whole the distinctively Jewish literature, from the beginning of our era to the present time, is hardly more than a continuation of the legal work of the six first centuries. The old national creative power was essentially religious, and the creative period seems to have passed. The modern Reform is active in literature, but it is not Jewish at all in any proper sense of that term.

If we are to judge from present indications, the people of Israel, as a nation, have done their work in the world. But that work, contained in our Old Testament, is a great one. They have felt God's presence, and spoken in his name to all humanity. They have bequeathed to us an inestimable treasure. It is not merely from historical curiosity that we study their ancient writings, but also from reverent desire to know God.

QUESTIONS.

1. What are the earliest Israelitish writings that we know of? What is their general character?

2. Why did the Israelites grow in literary power from the eighth century B.C. on? What sort of books were now composed? What advance in thought is marked by the rise of historical writing? What is meant by the pragmatic way of writing history?

3. When did Ezra live, and what did he do? What is a sacred Canon? When was the legal Canon formed? — when the prophetical?

4. What books were written by the sages or wise men? What was their object? What is the date and purpose of Chronicles? What books were written in the Maccabean period? When was the third Canon formed? What is meant by apocryphal books?

5. After the Maccabean period, into what study did the Jews throw themselves? Has this study produced anything new or of special religious importance?

LESSON I.

THE BEGINNINGS OF HEBREW HISTORY.

1. The Races of the Earth. — The nations of the earth, so far as we now know them, are divided into various races, which may be roughly named: American, Mongolian, Malay-Polynesian, Negro, and Caucasian. The Caucasian race embraces the Hamitic, Semitic, and Indo-European families. The ancient peoples who dwelt in the north of Africa, the Egyptians, Cushites, and Libyans, are Hamites; the Hebrews and their kinsfolk, such as the Assyrians, the Aramæans or Syrians, the Phœnicians, the Canaanites, and the Arabs, are the Semites; and the Hindus, the Persians, the Greeks, the Romans, the Russians, the Germans, the English, the French, the Irish, and other peoples of Western Europe are the Indo-Europeans.

2. The Migrations of the Semites. — In historical times the Semites occupied Western Asia, from the Tigris-Euphrates valley (Mesopotamia) to the strait of Bab-el-Mandeb. But in still earlier times a large part of them dwelt, along with other nations, in Mesopotamia and the adjoining country, and here probably lived the ancestors of the Hebrews. In those days it was not unusual for tribes to leave their country and seek other abodes, where they could have more room and more easily find sustenance, just as people came, and still come, from Europe to settle in America, and as now many persons go to the west of this country to live. So, at a very early date, one Semitic tribe travelled away, and settled on the shore of the Mediterranean Sea, and founded the cities of Sidon and Tyre; these were the Phœnicians. Not far from the same time other Semitic tribes came into the same region, and took possession of the land of Canaan, expelling or destroying the people they found there. These new-comers were the tribes that are called Canaanites in the Old Testament; such as the Jebusites, the Amorites, the Hivites, and the Perizzites. They dwelt in Sodom and Gomorrah, and many other cities. Probably about the same time came the Philistines, who were somehow connected with the Canaanites; but it is uncertain from what region they entered Canaan. Who the older tribes who preceded the Canaanites in this land were, we do not know. Some time after the Canaanites had settled there, perhaps about the year B.C. 2000, came another migration, that of the tribes that we call Hebrews. Besides the Israelites, this group of tribes included the Edomites, the Ammonites, the Moabites, and perhaps the Amalekites and some others. Probably these did not all come at the same time. It is likely that the Israelites themselves were made up of several different though closely related bodies of immigrants, who, in the course of centuries, were welded together into one nation; for a long time after they settled in Canaan, Judah and Ephraim held aloof from each other, and quarrels and wars often occurred between them.

3. The Nomadic Life of the Hebrews in Canaan. — At first the Hebrews wandered about with their flocks and herds in the southern half of Canaan, and perhaps in the country east of the Jordan. Gradually the tribes settled down in various parts of the land, all except the Israelites, who, as we shall see, before they came to rest in permanent habitations, were to spend some time on the borders of Egypt. During this period of wandering or nomadic life they had no regular government. Each small tribe had its chief, and probably each subdivision of a tribe had its elders, who exercised a sort of control over its movements, and administered justice. The laws in use were no doubt such as we commonly find among the wandering tribes of the desert. For the most part each man had to look out for himself. If a man was killed, his next of kin had the right and was expected to kill the slayer. The penalty of theft was double or fourfold restitution. Property consisted wholly of flocks and herds. There were no books among them; whether they were acquainted with writing is doubtful. Purchases of goods were probably made frequently by barter, though it is not unlikely that they had money of uncoined silver which was estimated by weight. The best picture of their life is to be found in that of the wandering tribes of the Arabian desert to-day.

4. The Earliest Form of the Religion of Israel in Canaan. — We should not expect that the religion of such half-civilized tribes would be very pure. God had great designs for these Israelites: in after years they were to become the teachers of the world in the knowledge of God; he was to lead them along a wonderful way. But their growth was to be slow. As it required many ages for our earth to reach a condition in which it should be habitable for man, so it required many centuries before the religion of Israel attained the form in which it could minister to man's highest needs, and prepare the way for Jesus the Christ. Before reaching full age the people had to pass through childhood; and it is of its childhood that we are now speaking, — we might say, of its infancy. At this stage of its life Israel differed hardly at all, at least in outward appearance, from its heathen neighbors. All these tribes had formerly worshipped stocks and stones, — dead things in which they believed gods dwelt. The Israelites had almost outgrown this, but still they had the custom of setting up sacred stones, and worshipping under sacred trees, as the Druids in England used to do. Old habits cling long to nations, as they do to us all. However, the Israelites had, by this time, got to the worship of gods who were mostly connected with the visible heavens and the heavenly bodies. This was idolatry, but it was better than worshipping stones. The broad sky, the terrible thunder-storm, the sun, the moon, the stars, — all these suggested to them divinities who dwelt in and governed these objects. We know very little about the names and characters of these gods. "El" was probably a general name for divine persons. One deity seems to have been called Elyon, which means "high;" another, Shaddai, the "mighty," or the "destroyer." There was perhaps a Gad, the god of fortune; and an Asher, the god of prosperity. Perhaps, too, at this time, they worshipped Yahwe (Jehovah), who afterwards became their only God.

5. Their Worship. — Like all other ancient nations they sacrificed to the gods, the offerings being animals (sheep, goats, bullocks, calves, pigeons), or wheat, oil, and wine. Priests, also, perhaps they had, though it is likely that every father of a family acted as priest in his own household. They had no temple, but built altars wherever they chose. Their worship was of the simplest kind, and they had no sacred books.

6. Their Language. — Their language was that which we call Hebrew, the language in which the Old Testament was written. It belongs to the same family with the Assyrian, the Syriac, and the Arabic; and it is altogether different from Greek, Latin, German, French, and English.

LITERATURE.

1. On the stories of Abraham, Isaac, and Jacob, in the book of Genesis: "The Sunday-School Primer on the Legendary Material of the Old Testament." They are legendary accounts which grew up among the people, and were committed to writing in later times. They represent later religious ideas, and embody many noble truths; but they contain only a small kernel of history. Vigouroux's "La Bible et les Découvertes Modernes," 2 vols., Paris, 1877, opposes the conclusions of Kuenen, Lenormant, and others.

2. On the various forms of religion, as fetishism, astrolatry, &c.: C. P. Tiele's "Outlines of the History of Religions," London, 1877.

3. On the earliest form of the Israelitish religion: Tiele's "Histoire Comparée des Anciennes Religions de l'Egypte et des Peuples Sémitiques," French translation, Paris, 1882.

4. On the connection between the Hebrews and Mesopotamia: Schrader's "Die Keil-inschriften und das Alte Testament," Giessen, 1883; Lenormant's "Les Origines de l'Histoire," &c., 2 vols., Paris, 1880, 1882, and English translation of vol. i., N.Y., 1882; George Smith's "Chaldean Genesis," edited by Sayce; and Duncker's "History of Antiquity," English translation, 4 vols., London, 1877.

5. For later stories of the patriarchs: Baring-Gould's "Legends of Old-Testament Characters," London and New York, 1871; Weil's "Biblical Legends of the Mussulmans," English translation, New York, 1863.

QUESTIONS.

1. Name the races of the earth. What are the three Caucasian families? What nations compose the Semitic family?

2. Where did the Semites live in the earliest times? Why did they move westward? Which of the Semites first came to Canaan? About what time did the Israelites first enter Canaan? What nations were their nearest kinsfolk, that is, what nations besides the Israelites were included under the name Hebrews? Were the Israelites made up of several different bodies of immigrants? Did it require time to weld these together?

3. What is a nomadic life? What sort of government did the Hebrews have at first? What laws? What sort of property? How did they buy and sell? Did they have books? What people now resemble them?

4. Were the Israelites destined to accomplish a great work? Did the religion of Israel have to grow as a child grows to be a man? Did the people at first worship stocks and stones? Afterwards, what gods did they have? In this early period did they worship Yahwe?

5. Did the Israelites at first have temples? — priests? What sacrifices did they offer?

6. What language did they speak? Is it like English?

LESSON II.

THE ISRAELITES IN EGYPT.

1. The Greatness of the Egyptians. — In those early times, namely, about B.C. 2000–1200, the Egyptians were the greatest nation of the world. They had already been a settled people, with a regular kingly government, for many centuries, perhaps from as far back as about B.C. 4000; and now they had a flourishing civilization, and a remarkable and, in some respects, noble system of religion. They had conquered most of the tribes dwelling around them in Africa, and carried their arms into Asia, along the shore of the Mediterranean Sea and eastward up to the Euphrates; they had built pyramids, temples, and palaces; their wise men studied art and science, and wrote books, for the Egyptians had invented or developed a system of writing (the hieroglyphic) sufficient for the expression of all their ideas.

2. The Fertility of Egypt. Dependence of the Desert Tribes on it. — Ancient Egypt was so fertile, thanks to the annual overflow of the Nile, that it was considered the granary of Western Asia, as it was, in later times, of Rome; it seemed to produce corn enough for all the world. In those days, however, there was little commerce, and it often happened that in times of scarcity of provisions, a tribe, instead of sending ships or caravans, would leave its home and go where it could find food. So it was with the wandering tribes who dwelt just east of Egypt on the borders of the Arabian desert. Their country was not very productive, they had only rude means of tilling the soil, and they were not infrequently exposed to the danger of famine. At such times they would move nearer to Egypt, where they could exchange their flocks and herds for wheat. The Egyptians, on their part, were not sorry to have friendly tribes settled on their northeastern border, for these served as an out-post and a protection against the bedawin (desert-tribes) and other Asiatic peoples with whom Egypt was often at war. These visiting tribes became dependent allies of the Egyptians, with whom they naturally entered into more or less close relations; we find accounts in the Egyptian writings of bedawin chiefs who attained high position in the Egyptian government. But it is probable that such tribes would give up their old habits and lose their distinctive character, in proportion as they became united with their more civilized neighbors.

3. The Israelites in Goshen. — It seems that among others the Israelites were driven down into Egypt by famine. It is possible that this happened more than once; for, in Gen. xii. 10, it is said that Abraham went thither when there was a grievous famine in the land of Canaan. This, however, would be only a passing visit; at a later period the people went to stay. Of this we have an account in the book of Genesis (chapter xlvi.), and there is no reason to doubt its general correctness, though the migration may not have happened exactly as it is there narrated. Instead of a family (Jacob's), moving into the land by invitation of the viceroy or chief officer (Joseph), we must rather think of them as a tribe wandering from place to place, and coming at last, as other tribes did, to the fertile region of Goshen, where they were allowed to settle by the Egyptian government. It may be that one of their number became a great officer under the king, and that this fact prolonged their stay in Egypt. But, according to our present information, this must be looked on as uncertain. These stories in Genesis were committed to writing long after those times, when the memory of the events was not clear, and additions had been made to the original facts, as so commonly happens in popular traditions. All that we need say is that, whether or not the beautiful and instructive story of Joseph is simple history, the Israelites did probably go to live in Goshen. We do not know certainly at what time they went, or how long they stayed, or what happened to them there, or how they came to go back to Canaan. The situation of the land of Goshen, where they are said to have lived, is also uncertain; but it was probably the border-land between Egypt and Canaan and Arabia, and large enough to furnish pasturage for the Israelites and for such other tribes as may have been dwelling there at the same time. This region was admirably suited for pastoral life, and we know from Egyptian accounts that it was occupied by pastoral tribes.

4. How the Israelites lived in Goshen. — We may suppose that the mode of existence of the Israelites in Goshen was not materially different from what it had been in Canaan. They fed their flocks and cultivated the ground, and occasionally, perhaps, made marauding expeditions into the neighboring regions of Arabia and Canaan. They would probably intermarry somewhat with the other pastoral tribes, and with the Egyptians. But they seem to have substantially preserved their own habits and institutions. We find in their later history almost no traces of borrowing from the Egyptians, which they would probably have done if they had lived in close social intercourse with them. It seems more likely, therefore, that they remained separate from their neighbors, and retained the social laws and religious customs which they brought with them from Canaan, as has been described in Lesson I. In the next Lesson we shall speak more particularly of their religious history at this time, but here we must mention one custom which they possibly took from the Egyptians, that is, the institution of circumcision, which was afterwards to become so important a part of their religious life. This custom existed among the Egyptians (though to what extent we do not know), and also among other African peoples, while the Israelites seem to have been the only Canaanite people who practised it. It is found among the Arabs after the beginning of our era, but it is not known when they adopted it. We know of no Asiatic people from whom the Israelites could have got it, and so it seems likely that they took it from the Egyptians, perhaps during that first visit to Egypt which is hinted at in the story of Abraham (Gen. xii.). At any rate, the custom was already established among them when they departed from Egypt to return to Canaan, and succeeding times regarded it as having been enjoined on the stem-father Abraham by God (El-Shaddai, Gen. xvii.). On some other things possibly borrowed from the Egyptians, see Lesson III. 4.

5. The Israelites forced into Hard Labor by the Egyptians. — At first, as it would seem, the Egyptians left their pastoral neighbors to themselves. But after a while the Egyptian king, according to the Israelitish account (Ex. i.), determined to make use of them in certain great public works in which he was engaged, and accordingly pressed them into service to aid in the building of several cities. From the name of one of these cities, Rameses (Ex. i. 11) it has been conjectured that the king who thus forced the Israelites into hard labor was Rameses II. of the nineteenth dynasty, one of the most famous of the Egyptian princes. He was a great builder, and the general circumstances of his reign are not unfavorable to the supposition that his allies were forced to become his workmen. If this view is correct, we may put the beginning of the oppression somewhere near the year 1400 B.C., and we may suppose that it lasted sixty or eighty years, into the reign of Menephtah, the son and successor of Rameses. It was during this period that, according to the account in Exodus (chapter ii.), Moses, the future deliverer of his people, was born.

LITERATURE.

1. On the history and manners and customs of Egypt: Brugsch's "History of Egypt," English translation, London, 1879, gives numerous extracts from the Egyptian inscriptions; Duncker's "History of Antiquity" is a convenient and generally sound work; Rawlinson's "History of Egypt," 2 vols., London and New York, 1881, is well arranged and clear, but not always reliable; Wilkinson's "Ancient Egyptians," London, 1878, gives full details of manners and customs. Other books are Chevallier and Lenormant's "Ancient History of the East," 2 vols.; Maspero's "Histoire Ancienne des Peuples de l' Orient," Paris, 1875.

2. On the Egyptian religion: the works of Wilkinson, Duncker, and Rawlinson above mentioned (Rawlinson's explanations are generally unsatisfactory); Le Page Renouf, Hibbert Lectures, 1879, "The Religion of Ancient Egypt;" Tiele's "Histoire Comparée" (mentioned in Lesson I.), and his "Egyptian Religion," 1882 (in the English and Foreign Philosophical Library).

3. On the Egyptian language and literature: "Hieroglyphic Grammar" in vol. v. of Bunsen's "Egypt's Place in Universal History," English translation, London, 1867; Brugsch's "Grammaire Hiéroglyphique," Leipzig, 1872, and Woerterbuch, Leipzig, 1867–1881; Renouf's "Elementary Grammar," London, 1875; "Funereal Ritual," in Bunsen, vol. v. above mentioned;

"Records of the Past," vols. 2, 4, 6, 8, 10, 12, London, 1874-1881, translations of Egyptian texts.

QUESTIONS.

1. At what time were the Egyptians the greatest nation of the world? What territory had they conquered and overrun? What had they built? — and written?

2. Why did the bedawin go to Egypt for food? If they settled on the border, what was their relation to the Egyptians? Would they learn something of Egyptian civilization?

3. Did the Israelites go to live near Egypt? Do we know exactly when and how they went? — or exactly where Goshen was? Do you know the story of Joseph? Are we sure that it is exact history? When were these traditions committed to writing? Was the country on the border suited to a pastoral life?

4. What were the occupations of the Israelites in Goshen? Did they intermarry with their neighbors? Did they borrow any customs from the Egyptians?

5. Did the Egyptians at first interfere with the Israelites in Goshen? Why did they afterwards force them to work? What labor were they made to perform? Do we know how long this oppression lasted?

LESSON III.

THE EXODUS AND MOSES.

1. Bible Account of Moses and the Exodus. — We may probably look on it as an historical fact that the Israelitish tribes at a certain time (perhaps about B.C. 1330) left the frontiers of Egypt, and made their way towards Canaan; but we know little of the particulars of the movement. The story in Exodus (chapters ii. - xiv.) tells us of the event as pious Israelites long afterwards thought of it, but we cannot be sure that their recollection was correct. Many of the particulars given in the narrative are improbable. God did indeed lead them out, though not in the way there described. According to the Israelitish account, Moses, hidden while an infant by his parents to save him from the king's cruel command that all Hebrew male children should be put to death, was found and adopted by the king's daughter, brought up in the court, and, it was afterwards added, educated in all Egyptian learning (Acts vii. 22). But, when he was forty years old, having killed an Egyptian officer who was maltreating a Hebrew, he had to fly for his life. He took refuge in Midian, on the east of Egypt, where he married the daughter of the priest Jethro, and remained forty years engaged in tending his father-in-law's flocks. At the end of that time he was sent by God back to Egypt to bring his people out. Here, with his brother Aaron, he called down ten terrible plagues on the Egyptians, and so forced them to let the Israelites go. He led them forth, first to Mount Sinai in Arabia, where he received the Law from God (books of Exodus, Leviticus, and Numbers) and gave it to the people ; thence they wandered nearly forty years in the wilderness (book of Numbers) after which they approached Canaan on the east of the Jordan, Moses made a farewell address (book of Deuteronomy) and, just before the people crossed the river, ascended Mount Pisgah, and there died alone and was buried by God.

2. The Exodus and the March to Canaan. — There are many reasons why we cannot think that this narrative gives a veritable history of the events ; some of these reasons will appear in the course of our Lessons. Yet we must suppose that the Israelites somehow reached the land of Canaan, and conquered it, and that Moses was really a great leader and instructor of his countrymen. It is not very important for us to know exactly what he did, and what the history of the Israelites was during their march to Canaan. This is the period of their childhood, and we shall be more interested in studying their later years. So for the present we may be satisfied with saying that the tribes probably led a nomadic life for some years, during which time Moses taught them as he had opportunity, organizing their civil and religious institutions, and preparing them for their succeeding life in Canaan. It is hard to say how long they wandered about before entering their new abode, — it may have been two years, it may have been forty, — but it seems to have been long enough to mould them in some fashion into one people. It does not appear that they gained many new religious ideas during this time. But here we must say a word about Moses and his work.

3. The Traditional Account of the Origin of the Law of Israel. — As our Old Testament is now arranged, Moses is represented as having received from God and given to his people at Sinai nearly the whole of the religious law by which they were guided down to the time of the coming of Christ. This is contained in the books of Exodus, Leviticus, and Numbers; then in Deuteronomy we find certain additions which he is said to have given thirty-eight years later, on the eastern bank of the Jordan. But we cannot take the account literally. The book of Kings and the writings of the prophets do not represent even the best of the people as acquainted with the Pentateuchal legislation down to the Exile. The law grew up gradually, and hundreds of years after Moses, when pious prophets and priests gathered together the religious usages of their times, they thought that it must all have been revealed in the beginning by the God of Israel, and so they came to believe that their great deliverer from Egyptian bondage had received it all at once. But we shall see that the succeeding history does not bear this out. The beginning of Israel's life was feeble; we shall try to follow it out to its grand ending. We commence with Moses.

4. What the Early Prophets said of Moses. Whether he borrowed anything from the Egyptians. — In the days of the prophet Hosea, about 750 B.C., it was believed that God had delivered Israel from Egypt by the hand of one of his servants: "By a prophet," says he, "the Lord brought Israel out of Egypt" (Hos. xii. 13). Who this prophet was, he does not say, but we cannot doubt that he was thinking of Moses. The prophet Micah (about B.C. 710) represents God as saying: "I brought thee up out of the land of Egypt, and redeemed thee out of the house of servants, and I sent before thee Moses, Aaron, and Miriam" (Mic. vi. 4). The prophets, however, tell us almost nothing of Moses' life, and the story in Exodus is largely the tradition of a later time. We know very little about his religious faith and his teaching. It is uncertain how far he was acquainted with the religious ideas of the Egyptians. It has been supposed that certain parts of the Israelitish worship were borrowed from Egypt, as the ark, the dress and observances of the priests, and the Urim and Thummim which were worn on the high-priest's breast. This is possible, but we cannot say that Moses introduced them; they may have been adopted while the people were in Egypt. We cannot point to any ethical or religious teaching which probably came to the Israelites from the Egyptians. It is remarkable, for example, that the two peoples differed so much in their ideas of the future life. The Egyptians believed that after death men lived as real a life as on earth. They said that there were judges in the lower world, that every man was rewarded or punished according to his deeds in this world, — the wicked suffered terrible tortures ; the good, having been tried and purified, their souls reunited to their bodies, dwelt forever in the presence of God, in the enjoyment of unspeakable happiness. The Israelites, down to the time of the Exile (B.C. 585), thought of the underworld as a cold, cheerless place, where the dead wandered about, inactive, without pleasure or hope. They seem to have learned nothing from the Egyptians in this respect. Their belief was the same as that of the Babylonians and Assyrians in the old home in Mesopotamia.

5. **Israelitish Customs before Moses.** — Moses found the people in possession of certain civil and religious ideas and customs. Besides their simple government and their sacrifices (see Lesson I.) they had probably festival-days, especially in the beginning of spring (vernal equinox), midsummer, and in the fall (autumnal equinox) ; these afterwards became the Pesach (Passover), the feast of weeks (Pentecost), and the feast of booths or Tabernacles, and they correspond in season to the Christian festivals of Easter, Whitsuntide, and Michaelmas. In early times, as far as we know, the Hebrews had no midwinter (winter solstice) festival, corresponding to our Christmas. The Israelites also had a sabbath, a seventh day of rest from work, devoted more or less to religious observances. This they had perhaps brought with them from Mesopotamia, where

something like it seems to have been a custom of the old Sumerian-Accadians. Then there were festivals at the beginning of the month (new moon), and perhaps others. These and similar customs Moses would no doubt try to bring under the influence of a purer religious feeling. Whether he added new ones, we cannot tell. Of his higher religious work we will speak in the next Lesson.

LITERATURE.

1. On the life and works of Moses : Kuenen's "Religion of Israel," English translation, 3 vols., London, 1874 ; " The Bible for Learners," by Oort and Hooykaas, English translation, Old Testament, 2 vols., Boston, 1878; Knappert's "Religion of Israel" (an abridged statement of the views of Kuenen and others of the latest school of Old Testament criticism), English translation, London, 1877 ; Stanley's "History of the Jewish Church," Old Testament, 2 vols., New York, 1870 ; Tiele's "Histoire des Anciennes Religions," &c.

2. On Egyptian and other accounts of the Exodus of the Israelites : the histories of Brugsch, Duncker, and Rawlinson, above mentioned.

QUESTIONS.

1. Can you give the biblical history of Moses ? Is it reasonably certain that the Israelites at some time left the frontiers of Egypt ? What date is suggested for their departure ?

2. Who led the Israelites from Egypt to Canaan ? Can we suppose that all the stories about him in the Pentateuch (that is, the five books at the beginning of the Old Testament) are real history ? If they are not, may they nevertheless be instructive ? How did the Israelites live on the march to Canaan ? Did Moses instruct them during this time ?

3. What books of the Old Testament contain what is called the "Law of Moses " ? When did the Israelites suppose that this was given ? Was the law made all at once, or gradually ? Was it natural that people should think in later times that God gave all the religious law to Moses ?

4. What did Hosea say of Moses ? What did Micah say ? How long was this after Moses' time ? What things may the Israelites possibly have got from the Egyptians ? Did they get any ideas of the future life ? What was the Egyptian idea of the life hereafter ? What was the ancient Israelitish idea ?

5. What civil government did the Israelites have before the time of Moses? What sacrifices? What festivals? Did they have a seventh day of rest (sabbath)? Did Moses establish any new civil or religious observances?

LESSON IV.

MOSES AND YAHWE (JEHOVAH).

1. Yahwe, the God of Israel. His Original Character.—Though, down to the Babylonian Exile (B.C. 585–535), the Israelites in Canaan worshipped various deities, yet we know that, all this time, their real national god was Yahwe (Jehovah), and that after the Exile they gave up all others and served only him. At first Yahwe was only one deity among many. But, as is so often the case with things that go very far back in time, we do not know whence the name came and what it originally signified. It is almost certain that the right pronunciation is *Yahwe* and not *Jehovah*, and so we may call it when we are speaking of the deity that the Israelites claimed as their own, as the Moabites claimed Kemosh (Chemosh), and the Philistines, Dagon; when we mean the one God, the Creator and Father of all, as Israel afterwards learned to know him, we may call him The Lord, as the name is rendered in our English version. We must wait awhile before we can speak certainly of the origin and meaning of the name Yahwe. As far as our present information goes, it seems likely that it came from Mesopotamia and belonged to some deity worshipped there, though it never got wide currency except in Canaan. From various expressions in the Old Testament we may infer that Yahwe was originally a god of the sky, especially of the thunder-storm. This suits the fine description in Ps. xviii. 6–15 (2 Sam. xxii. 7–16) and many other passages, and the common Old Testament name, "The Lord of Hosts," that is, Yahwe, the ruler of the hosts of stars. In process of time this origin of the deity was forgotten, moral qualities were associated with him, his worship was purified, and he became the just and holy God, such as we see him in Amos and the other prophets; and finally he became the only God.

2. Whether Moses introduced the Worship of Yahwe. Whether he was a Monotheist.—In Ex. vi. 2, 3, some later Israelitish writer represents God as saying to Moses: "I am Yahwe. I appeared to Abraham, Isaac, and Jacob by the name of El-Shaddai, but I was not known to them by my name Yahwe." It appears from this that some Israelites in after times supposed that the worship of Yahwe did not exist among them before the time of Moses. As has just been said, it is more probable that this worship was very ancient. Nations do not easily change their gods; it is not likely that Moses could or would introduce a new deity. But, as the Israelites believed that he had made some great change, it may be that through his means the worship of Yahwe became more general, became, in fact, in a real sense, the national worship. This would not necessarily mean that no other deities were worshipped. Indeed, we find in the succeeding history that this was not the case. Not only did the Israelites adopt, in part, the religious rites of the Canaanites (as Baal-worship and calf-worship), but for a long time they had household gods (teraphim), as we see in the histories of Micah (Judges xvii.) and David (1 Sam. xix. 13), and in the writings of the prophets (Hos. iii. 4). Still less would it mean that there was only one God, that is, that all other pretended gods were nothing. This is what we believe, and what the later Israelites (about the time of the Exile and on) believed; but David and generations after him thought that Kemosh and Dagon and the rest were real gods, only not gods of Israel. Exactly what Moses' belief was, we do not know. Probably, it may be said, he thought, as people in his day generally did, that there were a great many gods, that each nation had its own deity or deities. But he wished Israel to worship only Yahwe. And, in point of fact, they did remain in general faithful to Yahwe, till at last they abandoned all others.

3. Is the Decalogue Monotheistic? — But does not the Decalogue (the Ten Commandments) require monotheism, the worship of one God? As to this, we must observe two things: first, the Decalogue appears to teach not that there are no gods besides Yahwe, but that none but him is to be worshipped by Israel: "I am Yahwe, thy God, who brought thee forth from the land of Egypt; thou shalt not have other gods beside me" (Ex. xx. 2, 3); secondly, we cannot be sure that it was Moses who wrote down these Commandments, as we now find them in the Old Testament. Indeed, it is almost certain that he did not write them; for there are two versions of them, one in Ex. xx. 2-17, the other in Deut. v. 6-18; and these differ so much the one from the other (namely, in the ground given for the observance of the Sabbath), that Moses could hardly have written both. So it is more likely that they were written down after Moses' time. If he wrote any commandments the record has been lost.

4. Moses' Work Uncertain. — If we cannot suppose that the Pentateuch (the "five books of Moses") is correct history, then we do not know precisely what Moses did for his people. Did he try to make them more humane as well as more spiritual? It seems that in those days they were half barbarians; was Moses a reformer like the Athenian Solon? It is hard to say. In the times of the Judges, the Israelites seem sometimes to have offered human sacrifices to Yahwe; so Jephtha is said to have offered up his daughter (Judges xi. 30, 31, 34-40). But they may have learned this from the Canaanites; it is not certain that they practised it in Moses' time, and we cannot tell whether he tried to abolish it. And as to gods, we do not know what other deities besides Yahwe the Israelites now worshipped (see Lesson I.), nor their customs of sacrifice, nor their ethical ideas. We infer certain things from the Old Testament, but our knowledge is not accurate or sure.

5. What Moses probably did. — From all that we do know, we are led to believe that what Moses did was rather to organize the people and give them an impulse in religion, than to frame any code of laws or make any great change in their institutions. In after years it became the fashion to think of him as the author of almost all the religious customs of the land, as the divinely appointed lawgiver who received his instruction (*Tora* the Israelites called it) from the mouth of Yahwe himself. But it is not very important for us to be able to say that Moses did just this and that. Under the guidance of God, Israel grew in wisdom, and worked out a great Tora, an instruction in righteousness; and it matters little to us whether it was Moses or somebody else who had the chief part in it. But it is probable that he was a great man, and did much for his people.

LITERATURE.

1. On the work of Moses: the books of Kuenen and Stanley before mentioned, and the "Bible for Learners;" Tiele's "Histoire Comparée," pp. 356 f.

2. On the origin and meaning of the name Yahwe: the Hebrew lexicons; Friedrich Delitzsch's "Wo lag das Paradies?" Leipzig, 1881, pp. 160 ff.; Tiele's "Histoire Comparée," &c., pp. 347–351; J. H. Allen's "Hebrew Men and Times."

QUESTIONS.

1. Did the Israelites worship many gods? Did they, however, have their own especial deity? What was his name? What does our English version usually call him? How did the Israelites originally think of him? How did they regard him in later times when they had better ideas of religion?

2. Did some later Israelites think that the worship of Yahwe did not exist among the people before the time of Moses? In what passage of Exodus is this said? Is it probable that this was so? What may we suppose Moses did in this respect? Where do we read that the Israelites worshipped teraphim? Would it mean that they believed in one only God? Did Moses probably believe in one God just as we do? What did he wish? Did they do this? Would this mean that no other deities were worshipped?

3. What is the Decalogue? Where is it written? What does it say about worshipping Yahwe? Does that mean that the Israelites believed in only one God? Did Moses write the Decalogue in its present form? What is the difference between its two forms in Deuteronomy and Exodus? Does it make any difference in the value of the Decalogue, whether Moses wrote it? [Certainly not.]

4. What is the Pentateuch? Have we any knowledge of Moses except from the Pentateuch? Is that certainly correct? Do we know exactly what Moses did for his people? Can you give the story of Jephthah's daughter?

Was that before or after Moses' time? Do we know whether the Israelites offered human sacrifices in the time of Moses?

5. What should we say that Moses did? What did the people afterwards think of him? Does it matter very much whether God taught Israel by Moses or by some other man?

LESSON V.

THE CONQUEST AND THE JUDGES.

1. The March from Goshen to Canaan.— After leaving Egypt the Israelites seem to have moved from place to place in the northern part of Arabia, where they spent some time before reaching Canaan. Their route is described in a general way in the books of Deuteronomy (i.–iii., and x. 6, 7), Exodus (xiv.–xix.), and Numbers (x.–xiv., xx.–xxii.); and there is a list of stations (an itinerary) in Num. xxxiii. But these were written so long after the events occurred that we cannot rely on their correctness. Whether, on leaving Goshen, they crossed the upper part of the Red Sea, or skirted the Sirbonian lake, or went some other way, there is at present no means of determining. There was in later times a firm belief among the Israelites that they had spent some time at Mount Sinai in the peninsula called by the Greeks and Romans Arabia Petræa, and that there the Law was given by God through Moses. We know now that it was not there that God gave Israel its law; but the people, or a part of them, may have stayed there awhile. Thence they marched northward towards the Dead Sea, and perhaps approached their new land in two divisions, one on the east, and one on the west of the sea. Of the first division, some (Reuben, Gad, and a part of Manasseh) settled in the pasture-land on the east of the Jordan; and others (Ephraim, part of Manasseh, and other tribes) crossed the river and occupied the middle and northern parts of Canaan. The second division (Judah, Benjamin, and Simeon) came in at the south, and took possession of that region. We cannot say certainly that this was their course, but there is some probability in this view. Having got a foothold in the land, they fought their way from place to place. They were often beaten by the various Canaanite tribes, but they grew stronger and stronger, and at last, after a considerable time, became masters of the greater part of the country. Fortunately for the Israelites, the Canaanites were not united among themselves, and so the invaders conquered them one by one. Besides, it seems probable that the people of the land had been weakened by the attacks of the Egyptians and the Hittites. (Compare the Saxon conquest of Britain.)

2. The Book of Joshua. — The history of the conquest and division of Canaan by Israel is contained in the book of Joshua, the latter half of which has therefore been called the Israelitish Domesday-Book (Stanley's "Jewish Church," i. p. 289). The historical books of the Old Testament are generally made up of extracts from earlier writings, the whole being then revised by the author or editor. So it is with the book of Joshua. It seems to contain some old traditions (xxiv. 2) and some early lists of places (xii.-xix.) ; but it was composed at about the same time with the books of Exodus and Numbers, that is, after the Babylonian Exile. We find in it religious ideas which were probably not established in Israel till this late period. Such are the references to the priests (iii., iv.) and the Levites (xxi.) ; Josh. i. 6, 7 is like Deut. iv. 6, 9, 40, v. 32, and Josh. i. 8 is like Ps. i. 2. So the book appears to be a late production based on some earlier traditions, and we cannot look on it as an accurate history of the conquest. The great general and conqueror Joshua is himself a shadowy character. He was probably an able military leader, though he did not make all the conquests ascribed to him in this book. For from the book itself and from Judges we learn that after his death much of the land remained to be possessed (Josh. xxiii. 4, Judg. i.).

3. The Time of the Judges. — As soon as the Israelites had settled in their new possession, they began to cultivate the soil, build cities, and form a more regular government. They had their elders and tribe-princes as before, but there was no ruler over the whole nation. The tribes were separate and not always friendly to one another. Those dwelling on the east of the Jordan led a pastoral life, and had little to do with their brethren on the west of the river. These latter were divided into two parts: the northern tribes followed the lead of Ephraim, and the southern the lead of Judah; and Judah and Ephraim were rivals. When any part of the country was attacked by enemies, the tribes of that region joined together for the time being for defence. They would choose a general to lead them against the enemy, and, after peace was restored, the general would become a judge or civil ruler over that part of the land; but other parts of the country would not obey him. So it went on for a long time, till Saul was made king.

4. **The Book of Judges.**—The history of this period, from the death of Joshua to the death of Samson and the rise of Samuel, is given us in the book of Judges. This book was probably written during the Babylonian Exile by a prophetic man, who gathered up the writings and traditions of his time, and then composed the history according to the ideas of the pious people of that day. When we come to examine it, we see that it naturally divides itself into four parts: 1. Some particulars of the conquest (i., ii. 1-9); 2. A religious explanation of the successes and reverses of the nation (ii. 10-23); 3. A history of various judges (iii.-xvi.); 4. Some special incidents of the period (xvii.-xxi.). Much of this is no doubt valuable tradition, though it is mixed with popular stories (legends) that are not real history.

5. **The Principal Judges.**—Several of the narratives in the book are very interesting. Once, when the northern tribes had been conquered by a Canaanitish king named Jabin, they were delivered by the prophetess Deborah (whose name means "bee") and her general Barak ("lightning") (iv.). This victory is celebrated in a very fine war-ode (v.), which it is said Deborah composed (but that is doubtful); one is sorry, though not surprised, to see that the ode praises the Kenite woman Jael for killing the Canaanite general Sisera, who in his flight had asked

and received the hospitality of her tent. Then came Gideon (vi.–viii.) who defeated the Midianites, and restored his country's independence. There was a popular movement to make him king, but it did not succeed. His son Abimelech (ix.) seems actually to have reigned a few years as king over a small territory near Shechem, his mother's native place. It was her Canaanite kinsfolk and countrymen that supported him. He left no successor. Jephthah (xi., xii.) was a rude border-chieftain on the east of the Jordan, who crushed the Ammonites, and also chastised the haughty tribe of Ephraim. The story of Samson (xiii.–xvi.) is so full of legend that it is hard to extract history from it. Some writers suppose that it is all a sun-myth, like the story of Hercules. It is possible that it is a mixture of history, legend, and myth.

At the end of the book we have two important narratives. The first (xvii., xviii.) is designed to give the origin of the idolatrous sanctuary at Dan in the north, whose priests, down to the Israelitish captivity (B.C. 720), were descendants of a grandson of Moses (xviii. 30, where for "Manasseh" read "Moses," as the Hebrew text probably has it). The second (xix.–xxi.) describes the terrible punishment inflicted by the combined tribes on Benjamin for a crime committed by some of its people.

6. Civil and Religious Character of this Period. — During this period the Israelites were still in a half-civilized state. They had no settled government, and there was much lawlessness and suffering. Their morals were such as might be expected in such a condition of things, — there were assassinations like those committed by Ehud (iii. 21) and Jael (iv. 21), debauchery like Samson's (xvi.), and other abominations (xix.). The ideas of religion were rude. The people worshipped ephods and images (viii. 27, xvii. 5, xviii. 30) and the Canaanite gods (x. 6), though Yahwe remained the national deity (xi. 24). Anybody might act as priest (vi. 26, xvii. 5), though that was the special function of the Levites (xvii. 13), and priests of the line of Aaron are mentioned (xx. 28). There were various sacred places, where the people met for formal sacrifice. The ark is mentioned as being at Bethel (xx. 26, 27). Human sacrifice was sometimes practised (xi. 34–40). There seems to have been little organization, civil or religious. It was a time of turmoil and preparation, out of which we shall presently see order and prosperity arise. How long it lasted is uncertain (see Lesson VII.).

LITERATURE.

1. On the book of Judges: commentaries of Bertheau, Leipzig, 1845, and Lange, English translation, New York, 1872.

2. On the religious history: the works of Kuenen, Wellhausen, Knappert, Allen, and others above mentioned, and article "Israel" in Encyclopædia Britannica.

QUESTIONS.

1. On leaving Goshen, in what region did the Israelites move about for some time? Can we tell their route with certainty? Did they dwell for a while at Mount Sinai? Was the Law given there? In what direction would they march thence to Canaan? Did it take them a long time to conquer the land? What circumstances helped them to conquer it?

2. What book gives the history of the conquest of Canaan? When was this book probably composed? Does it contain extracts from earlier writings? Are its religious ideas mostly those of the earlier or of the later times? Can you tell who Joshua was, and what he did? Do you suppose that he wrote anything in the book called by his name? Why, then, is it so called?

3. When the Israelites had settled in Canaan, what did they do? How were they divided by the river Jordan? (See the map.) How were those west of the Jordan divided? Which were the two leading tribes? Was there any ruler over the whole land? What was a judge? Was the country a unit?

4. What book gives the history of this period? By whom was it written? When? Into what four parts is it divided? Can you point these out in the Bible? Is it all real history?

5. What is the story of Deborah and Barak?— the story of Gideon?— of Abimelech?— of Jephthah?— of Samson? How many additional narratives at the end of the book? What is the object of the first?— of the second?

6. During the period of the Judges what was the character of the civil government of the Israelites?— of their morals? What did they worship? Who were priests? Where did they sacrifice? Where was the ark? What was the ark? [A sacred box, containing something, we don't know what.]

LESSON VI.

SAMUEL AND SAUL.

1. The Situation in the Time of Eli. — The book of Judges carries the history to the death of Samson; in the book of Samuel we are introduced to a new scene, and the connection between the two books is not stated. We find ourselves at Shiloh in Ephraim, where there is a sanctuary of Yahwe, of which Eli and his sons are the priests (1 Sam. i.). How long this place had been a centre of worship we do not know (Josh. xviii. 1 is of doubtful authority); it seems to have been resorted to only by the central tribes. At any rate, it is a sign that religion was becoming more orderly; all through the time of the Judges it had been quietly growing into shape. The ark was in the Shiloh sanctuary, which was not a tent but a house (1 Sam. iii. 3); people like Elkanah used to go up thither to sacrifice (1 Sam. i. 3); the priests lived in part from the offerings of worshippers (1 Sam. ii. 13–16); and the menial work of the sanctuary (which was afterwards done by the Levites) was performed by a sort of guild of women. The priest Eli (it appears that the rank of high-priest was not yet established) was also judge; perhaps he administered justice in one part of the country while Samson was fighting in another. The political condition was unfortunate. The Philistines had been for some time masters of the central districts of Israel (Judges xv. 11). This people dwelt on the sea-coast west of Benjamin and Judah; they were brave and warlike and more civilized than the Israelites; their language was like the Hebrew, their worship (idolatry) was like that of the Canaanites, but we do not know exactly how they came into Canaan.

2. Samuel's Life and Work. — Up to this time the history has been very dim, but now we shall begin to see more light. We have come to one of the great names of Israel, a man whom we can call a great teacher and reformer in religion. It is Samuel, of course, of whom we are speaking. He is said to have been born in the territory of the tribe of Benjamin (1 Sam. i. 1), and to have been brought up by Eli at Shiloh (iii.). On Eli's death he succeeded him as judge over central Israel. As a political ruler he seems to have been vigorous and efficient; he united the tribes to some extent, beat back the Philistines (vii. 13), and finally aided in establishing a kingly government.

His religious work was not less valuable. Not only was he a zealous adherent of Yahwe against the Canaanite worship, but he probably founded the order of prophets, who in later times were to be the chief instruments of Divine Providence for purifying the religion of Israel. Ever since the conquest the people had been constantly tempted to worship the gods of their Canaanite neighbors. These Canaanites were not perfectly subdued till the time of David and Solomon. They dwelt in the midst of the Hebrews, were their superiors in civilization, and their religious ceremonies were gay and attractive. What wonder that the poor Israelites often fell to worshipping the Baals along with their own god, Yahwe? But there was growing up in Israel a party who believed that the people would not be prosperous and happy unless they put aside all other deities and served Yahwe alone. Others thought that there was no harm in serving all these gods. And so there arose a conflict between the two parties. Now Samuel seems to have been the organizer of the Yahwe party; that is, he was so zealous for the God of Israel and so intolerant of all others that he became a leader, and those who thought like him would help him in his efforts to banish the worship of the Canaanite deities.

To aid in this good cause he formed schools or communities of prophets. For a long time there had been seers or fortune-tellers among the Israelites. Samuel himself was a seer (1 Sam. ix. 9–11); people paid him for telling them where to find lost things. There were also men who felt themselves moved by a divine being to speak and declare his will; these were the prophets proper. The Hebrew prophet was not chiefly a foreteller of future events, but a declarer of the divine will. At first there was much superstition mixed with their utterances; they used to excite themselves by music and pour out their words in a frenzy. After a while they came to speak more calmly, and what they said had more moral teaching in it. In Samuel's day there were companies of these prophets (1 Sam. x. 5), and he was their director (xix. 20). They may have existed before his time, but he seems to have made them more effective, and to have laid the foundations of the prophetic life of Israel. We must not suppose that there were at this time any men like Amos and Isaiah. The "prophets" that Saul met were probably little more than frenzied seers (xix. 24). But a beginning had been made.

3. The Life of Saul. — For some time the people of Israel had felt that they needed a stronger government and more unity than then existed. When they were attacked they had nobody to gather all the warriors and oppose the enemy. One part of the country was beaten because the rest was inactive. We have seen (Lesson V.) that there had been an unsuccessful attempt to make Gideon king. Finally the need became so pressing that the people clamored for a change, the elders met together to consult (1 Sam. viii.), Samuel agreed to their demand, and, through his influence, a Benjaminite named Saul was chosen king. He proved, on the whole, a very good ruler. He seems to have united the greater part of the land under his sceptre. He was for a long time successful in his wars against the enemies of Israel, including the Philistines (xiv. 47, 48); though he fell in battle against them (xxxi.), they were so weakened by him that David easily conquered them. He seems to have been a bluff, frank-souled soldier, generous, impulsive, and self-willed. He was afflicted with a species of melancholy, a disease that darkened parts of his life; it is described in the narrative as possession by an evil spirit from Yahwe (1 Sam. xvi. 14). He was also a decided worshipper of Yahwe; we read nothing of his serving other gods. He was fiercely zealous against the idolatrous wizards and necromancers (xxviii. 3). But after a while he quarrelled with Samuel, or rather, Samuel withdrew from him (xv. 35). Two causes of this disagreement are mentioned: Saul, as head of the nation, once offered a sacrifice himself instead of waiting for Samuel (xiii. 9-13); and he refused to destroy the king and the cattle of the Amalekites, as Samuel commanded (xv.). That is, Samuel, though no longer judge, wished to retain his former prominence and authority, and desired that Saul should be as ardent a follower of Yahwe as himself; Saul, on the other hand, was inclined to be independent. Samuel therefore withdrew and chose another king (David), who would better carry out his ideas. Saul seems to have been beloved by his people, and, notwithstanding his unhappy death, added no little to his country's prosperity.

4. The Book of Samuel. — The history of Samuel and Saul is given in the first part of the book of Samuel, which is now printed as a separate book called First Samuel. Samuel was probably composed by a prophet during the Babylonian Exile from older writings and traditions.

LITERATURE.

1. On the book of Samuel: commentaries of Thenius ("Kurzgefasstes Exegetisches Handbuch"), Leipzig, 1864, and Lange, English translation, New York, 1877.

2. On Israelitish prophecy: R. Payne Smith's "Prophecy a Preparation for Christ," London and New York, 1871; Kuenen's "The Prophets and Prophecy in Israel," English translation, London, 1877; Ewald's "The Prophets of the Old Testament," English translation; W. Robertson Smith's "Prophets of Israel," New York, 1882.

QUESTIONS.

1. How far does the book of Judges carry the history? Where do we find ourselves in the beginning of the book of Samuel? What religious worship was carried on at Shiloh? Who was priest there? Was he also judge? What was the political condition of the country? Who were the Philistines?

2. Who was the great man of this time? Where was he born, and where brought up? What did he do when Eli died? Was his religious work valuable? Why were the Israelites drawn into the worship of the Canaanite gods? What did Samuel think of this? What was the Yahwe party? Why did Samuel found communities of prophets? What was a prophet? What was a seer? Were the prophets at first moral teachers? What use

did they make of music? What good work did they perform in later times? In Samuel's time were there any such great religious teachers as Amos and Isaiah?

3. Why did the Israelites wish for a stronger government? What is meant by a strong government? Who was chosen king? Of what tribe was he? Was he a good ruler? Was he successful against his enemies? Was he a worshipper of Yahwe? What did he do to the wizards and witches? Why did Samuel withdraw from him? How did Saul die? Did he add to his country's prosperity?

4. In what book do we find the history of Samuel and Saul? When was it written? Whence its name?

LESSON VII.

DAVID AND SOLOMON.

1. Legends of Great Men. — We have now reached another great name in the history of Israel — Saul's successor, David. We shall find that, though he was truly a great man, the accounts of him that have reached us are exaggerated. So it is with the histories of Moses and Samuel, and so it commonly is with the lives of great men who lived far back. The people remember that these men did some remarkable thing, stories about them grow up from generation to generation, and in later times all things that are like what they did are ascribed to them. Moses was believed to have begun the Law, and then he was believed to be the author of all the laws. It was known that Samuel had something to do with the prophets and the king, and so it was supposed that he chose and established the first king, and was himself a prophet, like Isaiah. David was a successful warrior and a poet, and was afterwards represented as having composed half the Psalms of the Old Testament.

2. David as King and Man. — David was born and reared in the town of Bethlehem, in the tribe of Judah. He was a shepherd and a warrior, and, while still a youth, distinguished himself by his deeds of valor (for the story of Goliath,

see 1 Sam. xvii.). It seems that in some way he became
the head of a party opposed to Saul, and he had to leave the
country and take refuge with the Philistine king of Gath
(1 Sam. xxvii.). On the death of Saul he was declared king
by the tribe of Judah (probably about B.C. 1040), and after
some years of war established his authority over the whole
land of Israel. He then began a series of brilliant campaigns,
in which, with his famous general, Joab, he subdued the
Philistines and other neighboring tribes (Edomites, Moabites,
Ammonites) and extended his dominion to the Euphrates
River. He conquered the Syrians, and became an ally of the
Phœnicians (Tyre), but did not come into contact with the
Egyptians and Assyrians, these nations being then elsewhere
occupied. David was thus the founder of a mighty
empire; in his day there was, perhaps, none mightier. He
made Israel a united people and laid the foundations of its
future history. His method of governing was like that of all
monarchs of that time; kings were then accustomed to do as
they pleased. He was tempted into committing wicked deeds,
as many other kings have been. He was not above the cruel
customs of his day (2 Sam. viii. 2, xii. 31). But he appears to
have repented of his evil when it was brought home to his
conscience (xii. 13), and to have been humble under affliction
(xvi. 11, 12); though it must be admitted that his dying
instructions to his son (1 Kings ii. 5-9) were not in the spirit of
the New Testament. We must judge him according to the
light he had.

3. David as Religious Man and Poet.— David, like Saul,
was a devoted worshipper of Yahwe; and, so far as we know,
never worshipped any of the Canaanite deities. This does not
mean that he thought there was only one God (monotheism).
On the contrary, he seems to have believed that each nation had
its own god, and that in every land one must worship the god of
that land (1 Sam. xxvi. 19). But he preferred the god of his
own country. When he became king and had conquered the
citadel of Jerusalem (Zion), he brought the ark to his new
capital, having made a tent (tabernacle) for it (2 Sam. vi.).

In those days the ark was believed to be the special dwelling-place of Yahwe, and great reverence was paid it (1 Sam. iv.–vi.); it was a small box, but whence it came, and what it contained, we do not know. (For the contents of the ark in Solomon's temple, see 1 Kings viii. 9; for later ideas as to what the earlier ark contained, see Heb. ix. 4, compared with Ex. xvi. 33, and Num. xvii. 10.) David intended to build a temple for Yahwe (2 Sam. vii.), but was so constantly engaged in war that he did not find time. The priests, offerings, and feasts, and other religious arrangements were about the same in his time as under Samuel and Saul. David was not only a great warrior, but also an excellent poet; he composed a beautiful and pathetic elegy on Saul and Jonathan (2 Sam. i. 19–27). Many of the Psalms are ascribed to him in the titles, but we cannot be sure that he was the author of any of them. In later times, when he was looked on as the great hero and warrior-poet, it was natural that he should be represented as the composer of the hymns of the temple-service.

4. Solomon as King and Sage. — Solomon, David's son and successor, was the most magnificent of the Israelitish kings. The period of his reign may be put at about B.C. 1000–960. He inherited and maintained the empire of his father. He enriched himself and his people by foreign commerce, and adorned Jerusalem with splendid buildings. He entered into marriage alliances with many of the surrounding nations. But he alienated the northern tribes by heavy taxation, and prepared the way for the division of the kingdom (see Lesson VIII.). At the same time he was a patron of literature and philosophy. He attracted to his court the sages of Israel and the neighboring peoples, and was himself a sage (1 Kings iv. 30–34, x. 1–13). The wise men of those days spoke chiefly of matters of every-day life; they gave rules of conduct in the form of short, striking sayings (proverbs), drawing illustrations from trees, beasts, birds, reptiles, and fishes (1 Kings iv. 33). Three books in the Old Testament are ascribed to Solomon: Proverbs, Song of Songs, and Ecclesiastes, but we cannot regard him as their author. The second and third were composed long after his time, and so was much of the first; but it is not unlikely that he and the sages of his court uttered and arranged a good many of these proverbial sayings (called in Hebrew, *mashal*, " similitude ").

5. Solomon's Temple. — Solomon was not exclusively devoted to the worship of Yahwe; he paid honor to other deities. His foreign wives had temples for their gods (1 Kings xi. 5-8), and he joined in their worship; and so, no doubt, did the people. But he was an Israelite, and fond of splendor, and he built a magnificent temple to Yahwe on Mount Moriah in Jerusalem (1 Kings vi., vii.) This was a very important event in the history of the religion of Israel. Up to this time there had been no central place of worship, but now all the people would go to Jerusalem to worship in the great temple of their own Yahwe. From this time the outward part of the religion, the ritual, ceremonial side, began to grow; and we shall see that it did both good and harm. The priests of the Jerusalem temple began now to take precedence over other priests, and their power continued to increase till they became rulers of the nation (after the Exile). It is not said in the book of Kings that Solomon's temple was built after the model of the tabernacle described in Exodus; and, in fact, it is doubtful whether this latter ever existed.

6. The Books of Samuel, Kings, and Chronicles.—The life of David is given in the two books of Samuel and the two first chapters of First Kings, and that of Solomon in 1 Kings iii.-xi.; and there is another account in Chronicles, 1 Chron. xi.-xxix. being devoted to David, and 2 Chron. i.-ix. to Solomon. The difference between the books of Kings and Chronicles is this: Kings (which is a continuation of Judges and Samuel) was written by a prophet during the Babylonian Exile; it gives the history of both the southern kingdom of Judah and the northern kingdom of Israel (see Lesson VIII.), and its object is to show that the nation's prosperity was in proportion to its obedience to Yahwe; Chronicles was written by a priest or a Levite more than two hundred years later, it gives the history of Judah only, and its object is to show that the nation's prosperity was in proportion to its observance of the temple-service. Much that Chronicles says of the temple-service is not reliable. The life of David in Samuel contains some repetitions and obscurities, but is in the main trustworthy. The history of Solomon in Kings seems to be somewhat embellished. Such embellishments, however, are simply records of traditions; the historical books of the Old Testament (except, perhaps, Chronicles) are honest endeavors to set forth the facts of the history.

7. The Chronology. — The chronology of the history of Israel begins to be firmer in the time of David and Solomon, though it is by no means sure. Before this time the numbers given in the Old Testament seem to be based on a tradition that cannot be depended on; so that we have, for example, to try to fix the date of the Exodus by the help of Egyptian history. But during the period of the kings, the numbers seem to be taken from written records, and if we can fix some one point, as the capture of Babylon by Cyrus, we can then reckon back to Solomon and David, having the aid of the Assyrian monuments. The date of the accession of Solomon, given above in the fourth paragraph, is approximately correct; perhaps within fifty years

LITERATURE.

1. On David and Solomon: the general histories of Israel mentioned in former Lessons; articles in cyclopedias and dictionaries. For the legends, Baring-Gould and Weil.

2. On Solomon's temple: Fergusson's "History of Architecture," London, 1874, and his "Temples of the Jews," London, 1878; articles in Bible dictionaries.

3. On the chronology of this period: George Smith's "Assyrian Canon," London, 1875; Schrader's "Die Keil-inschiften und das Alte Testament," Giessen, 1883; W. R. Smith's "Prophets of Israel," sections iv. and v.; the commentaries on Kings and Chronicles; articles in dictionaries.

4. On the book of Kings: commentaries of Thenius ("Kurzgefasstes Exegetisches Handbuch") and Lange, English translation, New York, 1872; articles in dictionaries.

5. On the book of Chronicles: commentaries of Bertheau ("Kurzgefasstes Exegetisches Handbuch") and Lange, English translation, New York, 1876; articles in dictionaries.

QUESTIONS.

1. Are histories of great men of early times often exaggerated? Why? Was it so in the case of Moses? — of Samuel? — of David?

2. Where was David born? What was his early history? When did he become king? What lands did he conquer? Did he make Israel a great nation? How did kings in those days govern? Was David better than the people of his time? Does he seem to have lived according to the precepts of Jesus? How should we judge him?

3. Did David worship Yahwe alone? Did he think that there were other gods? Why did he prefer Yahwe? What did he prepare for the ark? Why did he not build a temple to Yahwe? Was he an excellent poet? Can you mention one of his poems? Is it religious at all? What religious poems are ascribed to him? Can we be sure that he composed any of these?

4. Who was David's son and successor? How did he enrich the nation? How did he alienate the northern tribes? How did he encourage learning? Of what did the wise men or sages of that time chiefly speak? What three books are ascribed to him? Did he write any one of them? What did he probably do as a sage?

5. Was Solomon a worshipper of Yahwe alone? Why did he build temples for foreign gods? What sort of temple did he build for Yahwe? Where? Why was this an important event in the history of the religion of Israel? What of the priests of the Jerusalem temple? Is it said in Kings that Solomon's temple was built after the model of the tabernacle described in Exodus?

6. What two accounts have we of the life of David? What two of the life of Solomon? When and for what purpose was the book of Kings written? When and for what purpose the book of Chronicles? Wherein is Chronicles valuable? Are the lives of David and Solomon in Samuel and Kings in the main trustworthy?

7. What is chronology? When does the chronology of Israelite history begin to be clearer and more certain? From what nations do we look for help in the chronology? Will it help if we can fix some one point? How near right is the date given for the accession of Solomon?

LESSON VIII.

WORSHIP OF THE CALF AND OF BAAL.

I. The Division of the Kingdom. — The united kingdom of Israel lasted only about one hundred years, under the three kings, Saul, David, and Solomon (about B.C. 1060–960). There had always been jealousies among the tribes, especially between Judah and Ephraim, even in David's time (2 Sam. xix. 41–43); they had never been thoroughly welded together into one nation. David and Solomon were of Judah, and Ephraim and the other northern tribes did not like their inferior position. The discontent was increased by the heavy burdens that Solomon laid on the people in order to carry on his great buildings and his splendid court. Moreover, he had incurred the enmity of the strict Yahwists by his permission of the worship of foreign gods; and, in the latter part of his reign, one of this party, the prophet Ahijah, incited an officer of the king, the Ephraimite Jeroboam, to revolt; Solomon detected the scheme before it was ripe, and Jeroboam had to fly into Egypt (1 Kings xi. 26–40). But on Solomon's death, when his son Rehoboam went to Shechem to be crowned, Jeroboam came back, and the northern tribes sent him and others as a deputation to the new king to demand a diminution of the taxes. He refused to grant their request; whereupon they withdrew, saying that they had nothing to do with the Judah-dynasty of David, and the Ten Tribes chose Jeroboam as their king. There were left to Rehoboam only Judah and a part of Benjamin, and the insignificant Simeon (1 Kings xii. 1–21, 2 Chron. x.). From this time till the fall of the northern kingdom (B.C. 720) our history falls into two parts; we shall study the parallel developments of Judah and Israel, the latter name signifying all the tribes except Judah, Benjamin, Simeon, and Levi. As there were twelve tribes besides Levi (Joseph's sons, Ephraim and Manasseh, counting as two), and as Benjamin (in which was Bethel) belonged in part to the northern kingdom, the latter is called the Ten Tribes.

2. The Dynasties of Jeroboam and Omri. — First, let us take a rapid view of the external history of the northern kingdom, from the accession of Jeroboam to the accession of Jehu, that is, about B.C. 960–842 (these dates are provisional). The throne of Israel was not stable; kings and dynasties rapidly succeeded one another. After Jeroboam came his son Nadab, but he was soon conspired against and slain by Baasha, who reigned in his stead. So Baasha's son was killed by conspirators, and civil war arose, and Omri was made king. He built a new capital, Samaria, and founded an important dynasty, of which the kings after him were his son, Ahab, and his grandsons, Ahaziah and Jehoram (or Joram). There were at first wars between Israel and Judah, in which the former appears to have had the advantage, as, indeed, it was the larger country, with the more numerous population; but in Ahab's time the two formed an alliance, the king of Judah's son marrying the king of Israel's daughter. More important were the wars between the Israelites and their northern neighbors, the Syrians. Since David defeated them these Syrians had been growing in power, and now became Israel's most dangerous enemies, frequently overcoming its armies in battle, till they themselves were conquered by the Assyrians (B.C. 732). See 1 Kings xii.–xxii., 2 Kings i.–viii.

3. Calf-worship and Baal-worship. — During this time many things of great interest happened in the religious life of Israel. The two most important of these were that Yahwe began to be worshipped in the form of a calf, and the Canaanite deity Baal was adopted by the court and many of the people. The calf-worship was established by Jeroboam at Bethel and Dan. He knew that if the people continued to go to Jerusalem to the temple, they would be tempted to give up his government and obey the king of Judah. Therefore he made a separate form of religion for Israel. He put the great feast of booths (Tabernacles) in the eighth month of the year (about our October) instead of the seventh, as it had before been. And he set up two golden calf-images to be worshipped; they were intended to represent Yahwe (1 Kings xii. 26–32). The people had never ceased to worship images, and so they easily accepted these. Besides, there had long been a sanctuary of Yahwe at Dan (Judges xvii., xviii.), and perhaps there was an image of a bull there; it is likely that this was not an old Israelitish custom, but borrowed from the Canaanites. Jeroboam allowed any of the people to be priests, not only the Levites, while in Judah the priestly office was coming to be confined to Levites. This calf-worship seems to have lasted till the fall of Samaria, B.C. 720 (Hos. viii. 5).

It was Ahab who introduced the worship of Baal and Ashera (where the word "grove" occurs in our English version, we must understand "an image or wooden pillar of the goddess Ashera"). His wife, Jezebel, was a Sidonian princess, and wished to have the gods of her own country, and her husband readily yielded to her desire. The people also had seen much of the Baal-worship among their Canaanite neighbors, and were not disinclined to it. It was only a small party who were in favor of serving Yahwe alone. So, as the king and queen and the great people protected Baalism, it prospered through the reigns of the Omri dynasty, and had temples and priests and offerings and feasts.

4. Elijah and Elisha. — But the party of Yahwe was not dead nor inactive. Though there seems to have been at this time no opposition to the calf-worship (which was Yahwe worship), there were many people who were displeased that foreign gods should be brought in and honored equally with their own national deity. Of course prophets were at the head of this party, and the principal leaders were the two famous men, Elijah and Elisha. These two were alike in their hatred of the foreign gods, but very different from each other in character and manner of work. Elijah was a stern man, who lived alone in the wilderness, only appearing now and then to denounce the idolatry or other wrong-doing of the king. and incite the people to vengeance on the priests of Baal (1 Kings xviii., xxi.). Elisha had a house in Samaria (2 Kings vi. 32), was milder of nature, mingled with the people (2 Kings iv. 8), and sought to lead them to worship Yahwe by instruction (iv. 23) ; only one thing that seems cruel is reported of him (ii. 23, 24). Many stories are told in the book of Kings of their wonderful deeds ; the people naturally thought that Yahwe had given his prophets great power. And in fact they did at last succeed in crushing Baalism in Israel (see next Lesson).

5. Political and Religious History of Judah. — During this time there was more quiet, though not more progress, in the southern kingdom, Judah. The family of David continued to occupy the throne. There were various wars, of course. When Israel first withdrew under Jeroboam, Rehoboam wished to attack them, but listened to advice and refrained (1 Kings xii. 21). In his reign also the Egyptians came up and pillaged the temple of Yahwe and the royal palace (xiv. 25). After him came Abijam, Asa, and Jehoshaphat; this last was the friend and ally of Ahab, king of Israel, and his son Jehoram married Athaliah, the daughter of Ahab and Jezebel. The next king, Ahaziah, son of Jehoram and Athaliah, was slain by Jehu (see Lesson IX.). Under Jehoram Judah lost Edom, which had been its tributary. There is not much to say of the progress of religion in the southern kingdom during this period. The worship of Yahwe was maintained by the kings, the priests, and the people at Jerusalem. But the Canaanite gods were also worshipped, with their impure rites (1 Kings xiv. 22–24). Down to Jehoshaphat's death the kings did not favor these foreign deities; Asa even degraded his mother from her position (the queen-mother, that is, the mother of the king, was the first lady of the land) because she made an image of the goddess Ashera (1 Kings xv. 13.). But Jehoshaphat's son and grandson, Jehoram and Ahaziah, the son-in-law and grandson of Ahab, worshipped Baal, probably through Athaliah's influence. Though there were no such great prophets in Judah as Elijah and Elisha, we know, from after events, that there must have been a strong party devoted to Yahwe, and opposed to the Canaanite gods. And presently we shall see that this party was active and vigorous.

LITERATURE.

1. On Elijah and Elisha: the commentaries and histories above mentioned; articles in cyclopedias and dictionaries. Mendelssohn's oratorio, "Elijah," fairly represents the spirit of the prophet and his work.

2. On the contemporaneous Syrian and Egyptian history and the chronology: the works of Duncker, Maspero, Rawlinson.

3. On the Phœnician history: Movers's "Die Phoenizier," Berlin, 1841-56; Duncker.

4. On the religion of Israel: the works of Kuenen and Tiele.

5. On the Moabite Stone, the inscription on which throws light on the history of the Omri dynasty and the religion of Moab, see "Records of the Past," xi. 165.

QUESTIONS.

1. How long did the united kingdom of Israel last? Under what three kings? Had the tribes ever been completely welded into one nation? How did Solomon increase the discontent of the northern tribes? How did he offend the strict worshippers of Yahwe? What happened when Solomon died? Who was the first king of the Ten Tribes?

2. What tribes did the kingdom of Israel embrace? Was the throne a stable one? How many of Jeroboam's family reigned? How many of Omri's family? Were the kingdoms of Israel and Judah at first friendly to each other? Which was the stronger? In whose time did they form an alliance? With what other nation did the Israelites have wars?

3. What two important events took place during this period? Who established the calf-worship? Where? Why? What deity did the calf represent? Did the people accept this worship? Was it old Israelitish, or more probably Canaanitish? Who introduced the worship of Baal and Ashera? Whence did he take it? Did the people readily adopt it? Did they also worship Yahwe?

4. Were there people who wished Yahwe alone to be worshipped? Did they suffer the calf-worship? To what did they object? What two men were the leaders of the Yahwe party? How did they differ from each other in character and work? Do you know any of the stories about them? Did they succeed in destroying the worship of Baal in Israel?

5. After Israel withdrew under Jeroboam, what family continued to reign in Jerusalem over Judah? Did they have wars? What nation pillaged the temple and the palace? Who was Athaliah? Did Yahwe continue to be worshipped in Jerusalem? Were other gods worshipped? What king deposed his mother for idolatry? Was there a Yahwe party in Judah?

LESSON IX.

THE FALL OF THE BAAL-WORSHIP.

1. The Contrast between the Worships of Israel and Canaan. — In the preceding Lessons we have spoken of a conflict between the Israelitish and the Canaanitish forms of religion; in fact, this conflict makes almost the whole of the religious history of the northern kingdom (that is, to B.C. 720, when it perished). These two religions differed not only in the names of their deities, but also in the character of their worships. It is doubtful whether Israel (the whole nation), when it entered Canaan, had any god but Yahwe; and his worship was mostly grave and severe, — it seems to have included human sacrifices at one time, but it had no gay and licentious features. The Canaanitish worship of the Baals, the Ashtaroth, and the Asheras did have such features; it was bright and joyous, and that was very well, but it was also sometimes debasing. And therefore the prophets of Israel had a good reason, besides their attachment to their own national deity, for opposing it; we cannot help sympathizing with them in this. Looking back now we can see that their opposition to foreign worships was God's way of bringing Israel to a purer idea of the divine nature, and it is largely to Israel that we owe such better notions of religion as we have.

2. Elijah and Elisha determine to root out Baalism. — The prophets feared Baalism, and rightly. It was spreading over all the land; the people liked it because it was joyous, and thus they were led by it into sin. In Judah it was popular, but in Israel it was adopted by the kings and the nobles, and was on that account more dangerous. So the prophets Elijah and Elisha resolved to root it out. They believed that this could not be done so long as Ahab or any of his descendants sat on the throne, and therefore they determined to overthrow this family. For that purpose they selected one of the high officers of the army, named

Jehu, whom they knew to be a strict worshipper of Yahwe, and advised him to revolt against the king (1 Kings xix. 16, 2 Kings ix. 1–3). The army, they knew, would obey the general, and the people were not friendly enough to Ahab's family to support it.

3. Jehu's Reform.— The plan was successful. One of Elisha's prophets anointed Jehu king, the army followed him without a word, and the dynasty of Omri was destroyed (2 Kings ix., x.). Jehoram, Ahab's second son, was at that time king of Israel; he was slain, and his mother, Jezebel, and all of Ahab's family, and also Ahaziah, king of Judah. This happened about B.C. 842. Then Jehu set himself to crush out the Baal-worship. He called a great assembly of all the followers of Baal in the temple of the god at Samaria, excluded all worshippers of Yahwe, and slew the Baalites. The kingdom of Israel lasted about a hundred and twenty years after this, but Baalism never again raised its head. The calf-worship established by Jeroboam continued, — it was really a worship of Yahwe; but the Canaanite gods troubled Israel no more as they had done. Some remnant of their worship there was (Hos. ii. 8), but it grew feebler and feebler and at last died out completely.

In his religious reform Jehu found an efficient ally in Jehonadab, the son of Rechab (2 Kings x. 15). These Rechabites were strongly devoted to the worship of Yahwe, and enemies of all Canaanitish customs. They even refused to live in cities, fearing the luxury of that sort of life; they dwelt in tents, did not cultivate the ground, tended cattle, and refrained from drinking wine. They were still in existence in the days of the prophet Jeremiah (Jer. xxxv.). No doubt there were many stanch servants of Yahwe who never bowed the knee to Baal (1 Kings xix. 18, xviii. 4).

4. The Dynasty of Jehu.— The dynasty of Jehu lasted about a hundred years. The chronology is uncertain just here; we provisionally put the accession of Jehu B.C. 842 (it may have been from twenty to thirty years earlier), and the death of the last king of his family, Zachariah, B.C. 740. The military history of this dynasty was, on the whole, glorious. Under Jehu and his son, Jehoahaz, the Syrians gained important advantages over Israel, conquering the territory east of the Jordan (2 Kings x. 32, 33, xiii. 3). The next king, Joash, was a warlike prince and subdued Edom and Judah (xiv. 7–14). His son and successor, Jeroboam II., the greatest Israelitish conqueror since David, restored the prestige of his country; his kingdom extended from the Dead Sea on the south to Hamath on the north (xiv. 25), that is, almost to the Euphrates River, which was the boundary in David's time. He seems to have overrun the Syrian territory. In his reign prophesied the prophets Amos, Hosea, and Jonah; but the Old Testament book of Jonah was written later. Jeroboam's son, Zachariah (xv. 8–10) reigned only a few months; he was slain by conspirators, and with him ended the dynasty of Jehu.

The most important political event of this period is the appearance of the Assyrians on the scene. This people had been growing in power for several centuries, and, having conquered their immediate neighbors, had begun to move towards Syria and Canaan. They had descended as far as Hamath and defeated the Syrians; and it was probably in part because the latter were thus weakened that Jeroboam II. was able to subdue them (2 Kings xiii. 5). And Israel also felt the strong hand of the Assyrian. It is mentioned in an inscription of the Assyrian king Shalmaneser (B.C. 812) that he received tribute from Jehu. Whether Jehu's descendants also paid tribute to Assyria we do not know. As yet the great northern power only hovered threateningly in the distance. The prophets saw the danger and warned Israel (Amos v. 27, Hos. ix. 3, x. 6, xi. 5); but the end was not far off.

5. Political History of Judah. — In Judah during this period there was much disorder and suffering. King Ahaziah joined his uncle Jehoram, king of Israel, in an unsuccessful attack on the Syrians at Ramoth in Gilead; the two kings returned to Jezreel and were both slain by Jehu. Ahaziah's mother, Athaliah, then seized the throne and put to death all the royal family except Joash, the son of Ahaziah, an infant a year old, who was concealed in the temple of Yahwe by his aunt, the wife of the priest Jehoiada. Having succeeded in keeping him hidden six years, they made a plot, killed Athaliah, destroyed the temple of Baal, and placed the boy Joash on the throne (2 Kings xi.). For many years the fortune of war was against Judah. Joash had to buy off the Syrians with the gold and silver treasures of the royal palace and the temple of Yahwe (xii. 17, 18). His son Amaziah was defeated and humbled by Joash, king of Israel (xiv. 8–14). According to the book of Chronicles, the next king, Azariah or Uzziah, was more successful, subduing the Philistines, Ammonites, and other neighboring nations (2 Chron. xxvi.); the book of Kings says nothing about this (2 Kings xv. 1–5). Uzziah was contemporary with the last of the Jehu dynasty in Israel. The Assyrians had not yet approached Judah.

6. Religion in Judah. — We have seen that the worship of Baal was maintained in Jerusalem by the Kings Jehoram and Ahaziah and Queen Athaliah. It was destroyed by Jehoiada, and we hear nothing further of it till after the death of Jotham, the son of Uzziah. Yahwe was zealously worshipped; his temple at Jerusalem was repaired by Joash (2 Kings xii.). However, there were high places all over the land where the people sacrificed (xiv. 4, xv. 4, 35). This was not considered wrong at the time; it was the worship of Yahwe. Afterwards it came to be thought wrong to worship anywhere but at Jerusalem; and so the writer of the book of Kings, who lived at that later time, always blames the kings for allowing the high places to stand. And we can easily see that they would lead to the worship of other gods than Yahwe. So, for example, Beersheba in Judah was the seat of an idolatrous worship (Amos viii. 14).

LITERATURE.

1. On the political and religious history, see the books already mentioned.

2. On Assyria: Rawlinson's " Ancient Monarchies," New York, 1871, vol. ii., 99–121; Smith's " Assyrian Canon," and the works of Schrader mentioned above.

3. Racine's " Athalie " will help somewhat in understanding the times, though it is much modernized.

QUESTIONS.

1. What conflict forms the greater part of the history of the religion of Israel? What was the difference between the two religions? Were the prophets right in opposing Baalism? Why?

2. What two prophets resolved to destroy the worship of Baal in Israel? In order to do this, what was necessary? Whom did they select as their instrument? On what did they count?

3. Was the plan of the prophets successful? What two kings did Jehu kill? About what time did this happen? What stratagem did Jehu employ in order to slay the followers of Baal? Did Baalism ever trouble Israel after this? What ally did Jehu find? What was the manner of life of the sons of Rechab? Why did they fear city life?

4. What is a dynasty? How long did the dynasty of Jehu last? Was it in general politically prosperous? Who was the most powerful of its kings? How far did his territory extend? What prophets lived in his reign? What is the most important political event of this period? Where did the Assyrians live? How far westward and southward had they come? Had they weakened the Syrians? What king of Israel paid tribute to the Assyrians? Did the prophets see danger to Israel from Assyria?

5. During this period what was the condition of affairs in Judah? After the death of Ahaziah what woman seized the throne? Who was she? By whom was she slain? Were Joash, Amaziah, and Uzziah successful in war? Had the Assyrians yet approached Judah?

6. Was the worship of Baal still maintained in Jerusalem? Was Yahwe zealously worshipped? Did the people all over the land sacrifice on high places? Why was this not thought wrong at the time? Why was it afterwards thought wrong? And, in fact, would it be likely to lead to idolatry? Can you mention one seat of idolatrous worship in Judah? Where is this mentioned?

LESSON X.

THE PROPHETS AMOS AND HOSEA.

1. Development of Israelitish Literature. — None of the books of the Old Testament, as we now have them, were composed earlier than the eighth century before Christ (B.C. 800–700). The Israelites were hardly civilized before the time of

Samuel and David, and not ready to write books for a century or two later. We find that nations usually begin their literary efforts with poetry, short songs commemorating festivals, battles, and other remarkable events. Then come annals, brief records of history and tradition. Next we shall probably find sayings and discourses of wise men (sages and prophets). Last of all we have law books, connected histories, long poems, and philosophical discussions. This was, in general, the course of the literary development of the Israelites, and in the Old Testament we have its final outcome. First there were short pieces like the well-song in Num. xxi. 17, 18, and then longer productions, as in Num. xxi. 27–30, Gen. iv. 23, 24, 2 Sam. i. 19–27, Judges v. When the kingdom was established, there were probably attached to the court officers whose duty it was to record current events (2 Sam. viii. 16, 17). The priests and the prophets also would occupy themselves with collecting and writing out the traditions of the early times. It was about at this stage that the Israelites had arrived when Jeroboam II. was reigning in the northern kingdom and Uzziah in the southern. Many traditions had grown up about Abraham, Isaac, and Jacob, and the deliverance from Egypt. Perhaps at this time short histories of the patriarchs began to be written, and brief sketches of later times, together with lists of laws. These books have all perished, but their substance is contained in our present Pentateuch and historical books.

2. The Different Sorts of Prophets and their Writings. — It marks an important turning-point in the history of Israel when the prophets begin to record their discourses. There had been prophets since the days of Samuel, and they had spoken much. But what they said had been confined to some passing occurrence; they rebuked kings for evil, or predicted disaster or blessing, or gave counsel in emergencies. The number of prophets was very great. Obadiah once hid a hundred of them from Jezebel (1 Kings xviii. 4), and four hundred prophesied at one time before Ahab (xxii. 6). They were not all in the service of Yahwe; Baal and Ashera had their prophets (xviii. 19). And the prophets of Yahwe were not all alike.

The predictions and discourses of some, as Zedekiah in 1 Kings xxii. 11, were the result of mere patriotic enthusiasm, or desire to please the king; while others, like Micaiah in the same story, were controlled by moral considerations, and would never promise Yahwe's favor to any but those who did right. Almost all the prophets whose writings have been preserved belong to the latter class. At first no record was kept of prophetic discourses; we have no books from Samuel, Nathan, Ahijah, Elijah, Elisha, and Micaiah. This was partly because the Israelites were not accustomed to writing in those early days, and partly because the sayings of the prophets were short ,and disconnected, and related to single, passing occurrences. But after a while came a different state of things. Israel advanced in civilization and culture, and composition was more practised. At the same time the nation came into closer relations with foreign lands, Egypt, Syria, Assyria. Dangers threatened it from these great powers. Its future became complicated and doubtful. Good and wise men began to ask what would become of their people. Their God, Yahwe, was powerful — why, then, did their enemies conquer or harass them? So they began to see that God was not only mighty, but also holy and just; if his people would prosper, they must be holy also. There arose men who felt themselves sent by God to deliver this message to the people, to tell them that they were suffering because they had forsaken the commandments of the holy Yahwe. They were the true prophets. Some of them delivered or composed long and vigorous discourses (sermons, we should call them), and these were written down and preserved.

3. Amos. — The first of the writing prophets in order of time is Amos (we have nothing from Jonah, 2 Kings xiv. 25). According to the superscription of his book (Amos i.1), he was a native or resident of Tekoa in the south of Judah, where his business was to tend cattle; he was not a menial, but the owner of herds. There were in those days schools or communities where men were bred to the profession of prophet, by which some of them used to earn their living; such men were often venal. Amos was not one of them. He had no professional education;

the word of Yahwe came into his soul with such power that he must needs leave his herds, and go and preach to the people (Amos vii. 14, 15); so the Apostle Paul felt (1 Cor. ix. 16). His prophecies refer to both Israel and Judah; but he seems to have gone up to Samaria to live, and to have addressed himself chiefly to the northern kingdom. It was while Jeroboam II. was king (about B.C. 780). Israel was comparatively prosperous, and Judah was in adversity. In both kingdoms there was injustice and other wickedness, and in neither was the pure worship of Yahwe maintained; Israel worshipped him under the form of a calf at Bethel and Dan, and Judah practised idolatry at Beersheba and elsewhere.

Amos's words to Israel are stern. After denouncing punishment on Damascus, the Philistines, Tyre, Edom, Ammon, Moab, and Judah (i., ii.), he turns to Israel, describes its ingratitude, idolatry, and injustice (ii.–v.), and predicts captivity and other calamity (vi.–ix.). But at the end (ix. 11–15) he says that Judah shall be established in prosperity as in the days of old, and Israel shall be restored to its land, and dwell there forever. Yahwe, who reveals his secret to his servants the prophets (iii. 7), will do this. Yahwe, he says, is lord of all nations, not of Israel only. Amos's style is vivid and bright. His prophecies (which were not all delivered at once) were probably collected after his death.

4. Hosea. — Hosea, who was a younger contemporary of Amos (about B.C. 775–725), also addresses himself chiefly to the northern kingdom. We know nothing of his origin and life; but we can see from his book that he was of a different nature from Amos. He pleads tenderly with his people to forsake their evil. His tone is one of loving sorrow. He sees that Israel must suffer punishment for its sin, but he grieves over the sad condition of things. He makes prominent Yahwe's love for his people. He has many references to the old times; he speaks a great deal of the patriarch Jacob especially (xii.). With all his tenderness he can be sharply severe; he does not try to excuse the people's sin : " Shall I ransom them from the hand of Sheol? shall I redeem them from death? Where are thy plagues, O death? where thy pestilence, O Sheol? repentance shall be hid from my eyes" (xiii. 14). In his days Assyria began to threaten Israel, and he predicts that they shall be conquered and carried away captive by this people (ix. 3, xi. 5). He closes with a word of love and promise (xiv. 4–8). Some man, who edited his book, added at the end an exhortation to the reader (xiv. 9).

5. The Influence of Amos and Hosea.—Thus these two prophets strove to hold their people to the worship of Yahwe alone. And more, they speak of Yahwe as a holy God, who will not endure wickedness. In this way they laid the foundations of pure monotheism. Perhaps they thought that the Baals and the other deities were real gods; but Yahwe they believed stood above them all in ethical qualities, and after a while Israel came to see that they are not gods at all, but only names.

LITERATURE.

1. On Israelitish prophecy: the books mentioned in Lesson VI.; W. Robertson Smith's "Old Testament in the Jewish Church," New York, 1881; Fairbairn's "Prophecy."

2. On Amos and Hosea: the commentaries of Steiner, 1881 ("Kurzgefasstes Exegetisches Handbuch"), Lange, and Pusey, and the "Speaker's Commentary;" Heilprin's "Historical Poetry of the Ancient Hebrews," New York, 1879, 1880; Duhm's "Theologie der Propheten," Bonn, 1875; W. R. Smith's "Prophets of Israel."

3. On the earliest writings: the Introductions of De Wette-Schrader, Berlin, 1869, and Bleek-Wellhausen, Berlin, 1878; Heilprin's work above mentioned.

QUESTIONS.

1. When were the earliest of our Old Testament books composed? How do nations usually begin their literary efforts? What comes after this? Was this the case with the Israelites? What men wrote down the annals and traditions? Did the Israelites perhaps have brief historical and legal writings in the days of Jeroboam II. and Uzziah? Do any of these older books now exist?

2. Did the earliest prophets speak much? On what occasions? Was the number of prophets great? Did other gods besides Yahwe have prophets? Were the prophets of Yahwe all alike? What was the difference between Zedekiah and Micaiah, for instance? Did the earlier prophets compose books? Why not? What change came about in Israel's literary culture and general condition? When Israel suffered, what did the true prophets say was the reason? Was it a great step forward when they began to talk about the holiness of Yahwe?

3. Who is the earliest of the writing prophets? Where was he born, and what was his business? Was he a professional prophet? Why did he preach? Where did he prophesy? Under what king? What was the condition of Israel at this time? — the condition of Judah? What is the tone of Amos's words to Israel? What hope does he hold out to Judah and Israel? Does he call Yahwe the lord of all nations? Is this an advance out of national religious narrowness?

4. What was the date of Hosea's prophecies? To which kingdom did he chiefly address himself? Was his disposition like that of Amos? What is his tone? What quality of Yahwe does he make prominent? Is he also sometimes severe? What does he say of Assyria?

5. What did Amos and Hosea try to do? How did they speak of Yahwe? How did they lay the foundations of pure monotheism?

LESSON XI.

THE FALL OF ISRAEL. AHAZ AND HEZEKIAH IN JUDAH.

1. The Fall of the Northern Kingdom. — After the death of Jeroboam II. (about B.C. 744) the kingdom of Israel rapidly declined. The throne was occupied for twenty years by a series of worthless kings. There were constant wars, intrigues, and murders. King Pekah of Israel twice joined the Syrians in attacks on Judah; the second attack, which was directed against Ahaz (about B.C. 734), failed completely (2 Kings xvi. 5, Is. vii. 1). Ahaz called in the aid of the Assyrian king Tiglath-pileser II., who in B.C. 732 captured Damascus and destroyed the kingdom of Syria. For about 230 years (that is, ever since the death of Solomon) the Syrians had been a thorn in the side of Israel. But Israel gained nothing by their destruction; they had, in fact, of late years been a barrier between it and the Assyrians, and now, the barrier removed, Israel was at the mercy of the huge northern empire. The end was not long delayed. In the year 729 B.C. Hoshea (the name is the same as that of the prophet Hosea) ascended the throne of Samaria. He was a well-meaning man, and seems to have struggled hard to maintain his country's independence. He adhered to the worship of Yahwe, and even attempted some reform (2 Kings xvii. 2). Seeing the overwhelming power of Assyria, he acknowledged himself the vassal of Shalmaneser (who was now on the throne), and paid him tribute. But soon after, he made the mistake of rebelling against Shalmaneser, and entering into alliance with Sabak (called in the Old Testament So), the Kushite king of Egypt. The Assyrians advanced against Israel, and in B.C. 720 Sargon, who had succeeded Shalmaneser, captured Samaria, and then inflicted a decisive defeat on the Egyptians. The people of Israel were carried away and settled in Assyria, while men were brought from Assyria and settled in Samaria and round about (2 Kings xvii. 24). So the Assyrians used to do with all the nations they conquered.

2. The Fate of the Israelites. — Thus ended the kingdom of Israel after an existence of about 240 years (B.C. 960–720). It had lived a troublous life, full of wars without and disorders within. It had produced strong religious men like Elijah, Elisha, and Hosea, and able kings, like Jeroboam I., Jehu, and Jeroboam II. But its religious career ended prematurely, before it had attained the knowledge of the one God. Its people, however, were not destroyed. Some of them remained in their own land and intermarried with the Assyrian colonists, and from them sprang the Samaritans, of whom we read in the book of Nehemiah and the Gospels. Others who were left in the land probably went down into Judah and settled. Those who were carried into Assyria settled there permanently. Some of them intermarried with the inhabitants and ceased to be Israelites. Others, no doubt, joined the people of Judah who were afterwards carried to Babylon by Nebuchadnezzar. Those of them who remained faithful to the religion of their fathers helped to form a distinct community which lasted hundreds of years. They had great schools for the study of their law. Here they remained till after the Moslem conquest, and then made their way into Egypt and Spain, and thence into France and Germany. The Ten Tribes are no doubt now represented to some extent in the Jews who are found all over the world.

3. Political History of Judah under Ahaz and Hezekiah. — Israel had passed away, but the kingdom of Judah was to remain for 130 years yet. It was saved from overthrow, first by submission to the Assyrians, and then by the fact that the latter were occupied by wars with Egypt and other nations. The reigns of Uzziah and his son Jotham (B.C. 780-740) were comparatively quiet. Then came Ahaz, who was attacked by the Syrians and Israelites, and called on the Assyrian king for aid. The latter helped him, and Ahaz visited him as his vassal at Damascus (2 Kings xvi. 10). In the year B.C. 726 Ahaz died and was succeeded by his son Hezekiah. It was a time that called for skill, decision, and bravery. The Assyrians were overrunning the whole of southwestern Asia, nor could the Egyptians stand before them. Hezekiah's only military hope was in the quarrels of his powerful neighbors and the strength of the city of Jerusalem. Against the petty peoples around Judah, such as the Philistines, he was successful in war, and in his later years he made an alliance with the king of Babylon (2 Kings xx. 12, 13), who was at that time (about B.C. 710 or 704) in revolt against Assyria. Some years later the Assyrian king Sennacherib overran the territory of Judah, and besieged Jerusalem, but retired when Hezekiah acknowledged his authority, and paid him a large sum in silver and gold. The Jewish king thereupon made a treaty with the Kushite (Ethiopian) Tirhakah, who then ruled over Egypt, and revolted from Sennacherib. The latter then again invaded Palestine, and, marching by Jerusalem, went to meet the Egyptian army. On the eve of battle, however, the Assyrian host was overwhelmed by some dreadful calamity (2 Kings xix.), the nature of which is not known, and Sennacherib returned home (B C. 701). Soon after this Hezekiah died (B.C. 697), and the land had rest.

4. **Religious History of Judah.** — Judah's religious history during the latter part of this century comprises two important events: a reaction by Ahaz, and a reform by Hezekiah. Ahaz re-established the old Canaanite custom of human sacrifice (perhaps it was also an old Israelite custom), and resumed worship in the high places (2 Kings xvi. 3, 4). Possibly in this he was imitating the idolatry of his friends the Assyrians; and the people would not be slow to follow his example. Seeing an altar that he liked at Damascus, he sent orders to the priest Urijah to make a similar one for the temple of Yahwe at Jerusalem (2 Kings xvi. 10-16). The priest obeyed, and the king prescribed the sacrificial service. All this was regarded as lawful worship of Yahwe; it seems that the strict rules of the book of Leviticus did not exist at this time. But when Hezekiah came to the throne everything was changed. Fortunately he was the obedient pupil of the prophet Isaiah, who was zealous for the worship of Yahwe. All images of gods and pillars erected to Ashera were destroyed. Among others there was a bronze serpent that had long been an object of worship, and was said to have been made by Moses for a particular purpose (Num. xxi. 9); Hezekiah broke it in pieces, calling it contemptuously *nehushtan*, "a bronze thing." He went farther, and removed the high places, where the people had worshipped Yahwe from time immemorial. This seemed to many persons a violent procedure, — it appeared to be breaking up the worship of Yahwe; and this was the report that the Assyrians had of it (2 Kings xviii. 22). But Hezekiah suppressed these local places of worship in order to force his people to come up to the temple at Jerusalem, where it would be possible to guard against idolatry. It was a step in the right direction; and though the next king returned to the old practices, and the reform was not completed for eighty years, Hezekiah laid the foundation of the work.

LITERATURE.

The commentaries on Kings and histories above mentioned, especially Lange, Schrader, George Smith, and Tiele. Also Cheyne's "Prophecies of Isaiah," London, 1880.

QUESTIONS.

1. After the death of Jeroboam II., what was the fortune of Israel? When Israel and Syria attacked Ahaz, king of Judah, whom did he call to his aid? What became of the kingdom of Syria? Did its destruction help Israel? Who was the last king of Israel? What was his character? Why did he submit to Assyria? What mistake did he afterwards make? What was the result? In what year was Samaria captured by Sargon? Is this date tolerably certain? [Yes, it is assured by the Assyrian inscriptions.] What became of the people of Israel?

2. How long did the kingdom of Israel endure? Did it produce great men? Did it reach clear religious knowledge? Were its people all destroyed? What became of those who remained in their own land? — of those who were carried away to Assyria? Where are they now? What would you say of attempts to find the Ten Tribes in various Asiatic, European, or American nations? [Such attempts are folly.]

3. How long did the kingdom of Judah last after the fall of Israel? How was it saved from overthrow? What was Ahaz's career? Who was his son and successor? When did he ascend the throne? Was Hezekiah successful against his petty neighbors? Was he obliged to submit to the Assyrians? What became of the Assyrian army?

4. What two important events occurred in this period? Describe the reaction of Ahaz? Was this then thought to be lawful? When Hezekiah came to the throne, did he follow his father's example? Who was his chief adviser in religion? What did he do to the images? — to the bronze serpent? What is the story about Moses and this serpent? Did Hezekiah suffer the high places to remain? Why not?

LESSON XII.

THE PROPHETS MICAH AND ISAIAH.

1. The Groups of Prophets. — The prophets were preachers, but preachers of a peculiar sort: their discourses were always addressed to the nation. They denounced its vices, and they looked forward to and depicted its future. Thus they were eminently men of their times, and the tone of their writings varies according to the changing outward and inward circumstances of the people. We may group them by historical periods, each period having certain political and religious characteristics: 1. The prophets of the Jehu dynasty, Amos and Hosea, when the fall of Israel was impending; 2. The Judah prophets of the first Assyrian attack, Micah and Isaiah I., after whom, at a later time, follows Nahum; 3. The prophets of the Chaldean period, Zephaniah, Habakkuk, Jeremiah, Obadiah; 4. The prophets of the Exile, Ezekiel and Isaiah II.; 5. The prophets of the return, Haggai and Zechariah I; 6. The prophets of the legal period, Malachi, Joel, Zechariah II.

2. The Times of Micah and Isaiah. — Before studying the writings of Micah and Isaiah, let us look at the circumstances of their time, and the ideas these circumstances gave rise to. Judah was now beginning to be a part of the great world. Heretofore it had been an isolated little land, warring with tribes around it, but mostly unknown to and ignorant of the great empires. Now approaches the time when it is to be absorbed into the world's history. It is to fall into the clutches of Assyria, and then into the hands of the Babylonians, Persians, Greeks, and Romans. In our survey of the history we have come to the starting-point of this process, — the first attack on Judah by Assyria. The question was, what to do. Isaiah and his friends said, "Keep clear of foreign alliances, trust Yahwe, and he will take care of his people;" but Hezekiah did not follow their advice. This was the burden of the prophets' cry: "We are Yahwe's people, and he will give us victory over our enemies, and peace and prosperity." And as the present did not offer this prosperity, they looked to the future for its incoming, and painted a glorious time of triumph and joy. In the different historical periods this time of joy was portrayed in different forms. The peculiarity of the portraiture in Hezekiah's time is that Judah's glory is expected to be ushered in by an individual king, a descendant of David. For the king was the natural head of the nation, and it was the house of David that God had placed on the throne. Afterwards this royal deliverer was called the "anointed one," or the Messiah (kings were anointed with oil at their coronation); and so we generally call this expectation of future glory for the people the Messianic hope of Israel.

3. Micah. — Of Micah we know only what is stated in the inscription of his prophecy (and we cannot be always sure that these inscriptions are wholly correct), that he preached in the days of Kings Jotham, Ahaz, and Hezekiah (perhaps about B.C. 745–702), with one little incident recorded in Jer. xxvi. 18, 19. He seems to have been a sad and passionate man (i. 8); it is vengeance on sin that he mostly speaks of. The outline of his book is this: after denouncing the sin of Israel and Judah, he describes a march of the Assyrians through the territory of Judah (i. 9–16), with many plays on the names of the various places; it is hard to say whether this march is real or imagined. Next comes a terrible picture of the wickedness of the people (ii., iii.), and then he turns to tell of the glorious time when many nations should give up their own gods and worship Yahwe, and wars should cease (iv. 1–5). Zion's enemies were then pressing her hard, and an Assyrian attack was expected, but the prophet comforts himself with thought of that king, of the ancient family of David, who should conquer the Assyrians (iv. 11–v. 8). In later times this was supposed to refer to Christ (Mat. ii. 4–6); but, though Christ was a great deliverer, it is not probable that the prophet is referring to him here. Micah's last discourses have much to say about holiness of life (see the noble thought in vi. 8). Society in his time was very corrupt, but he looks hopefully to God's mercy (vii. 18–20). Notice the references to the ancient times (vi. 4, 5, vii 15, 20).

4. The Life of Isaiah. — The prophet Isaiah is one of the greatest figures of the Old Testament, and his book one of the noblest, from the extent, vigor, eloquence, and lofty religious sentiment of its discourses. He had a long career, beginning in Uzziah's last year (Is. vi. 1), and reaching probably to the close of Hezekiah's reign, about B.C. 750–700. There was a tradition that he wrote the annals of Hezekiah's time (2 Chron. xxxii. 32). But it is as prophet and statesman that he is known to us. Disregarded by Ahaz (Is. vii. 12), he became Hezekiah's chief adviser (2 Kings xix. 2, xx. 1, 14), warned him against trusting to Egypt and other nations, and, on the occasion of Sennacherib's invasion, counselled him to resist the Assyrians and trust in Yahwe. For half a century his voice was lifted up against the idolatry and wickedness of his people, against religious formalism, for purity and holiness (see chap. i.). He looked steadfastly forward to the triumph of holiness in the triumph of the pure worship of Yahwe.

5. **Isaiah's Prophecies.** — The book of the Old Testament to which Isaiah's name is attached is a long one, of sixty-six chapters. But not all of this was written by our prophet. The second part, chapters xl.-lxvi., is the work of a prophet of the Exile, whom we will call the Second Isaiah (Isaiah II.). It is probable, also, that the historical chapters, xxxvi.-xxxix., which are interposed between the two parts, belong to the same period (though they may be based on notes made by Isaiah or one of his contemporaries); they are nearly identical with 2 Kings xviii. 13-xx. Of the remaining thirty-five chapters, we must leave out xiii. and xiv. 1-23, xv. and xvi. 1-12, and probably xxi., xxxiv., xxxv. There still remains enough to illustrate the prophet's genius and piety. Among the more striking discourses may be mentioned the call to repentance in chapter i., the woes, in v., the prediction of Assyria's overthrow, in x., and the picture of the days of the righteous king, in xi.; and the vision, in vi., and the prophet's symbolical children, in vii. and viii., are not less interesting. The discourses must be read not by chapters, but as wholes, and it must be remembered that Isaiah had in mind on the one hand Israel's political enemies, and on the other, the idolatry, formality, and wickedness of the people.

6. **Isaiah's Hope of the Future.** — And to what future did the prophet look forward for his people? He expected political independence and prosperity under a Davidic king. He speaks of a prince born or to be born in his own time (ix. 6, 7), under whom Israel should conquer its enemies, peace should prevail, Yahwe should be worshipped everywhere, and even wild beasts and serpents should become harmless (xi.). And there should

then be righteousness and holiness in the land. These hopes of the prophet were not literally fulfilled. Egypt was never united with Assyria in the worship of Yahwe (xix. 21-25). No son of David was ever after to be a conquering king. But in its broad scope what the prophet looked for has really come to pass. The purified knowledge of the one true God has been established in the earth. Out of Israel came Jesus of Nazareth, the Messiah, the Christ, who has taught us to worship the Father, and has founded a kingdom more glorious and enduring than was ever dreamed of by king or prophet. Isaiah's trust in God's righteousness and faithfulness was not a mistake.

LITERATURE.

1. On Micah: the general commentaries mentioned in Lesson X. 2; Noyes.

2. On Isaiah: Delitzsch's Commentary, English translation, Edinburgh, 1869; Cheyne's "Prophecies of Isaiah," London, 1880; Noyes.

3. Maurice's "Prophets and Kings of the Old Testament," Boston, 1853; Ewald's "Prophets of the Old Testament." English translation, London, 1875; W. R. Smith's "Prophets of Israel," New York. 1882 ; articles on Micah and Isaiah in cyclopedias; books of Introduction.

QUESTIONS.

1. What was the peculiarity of the prophets as preachers ? Do their discourses vary in character according to the times ? How may we group them ? How many groups ? Can you mention the prophets of each group ?

2. Before studying the writings of the prophets, what is it proper to learn ? When Assyria attacked Judah, what did Isaiah counsel ? In whose help did he trust ? Did Judah attain to prosperity immediately ? When the present did not bring peace, to what point did the prophets look? With what did the prophet's picture of future joy vary? What was its form in the days of Micah and Isaiah ? What is meant by the Messianic hope of Israel ?

3. What do we know of Micah's life? What incident concerning him is recorded in the book of Jeremiah ? What was his character? By whom

does he expect Yahwe to deliver Judah from the Assyrians? [iv. 2-v. 8.] To whom did the early Christians think this referred? Is this view correct? Can you mention a noble passage in Micah's writings?

4. Was Isaiah a great man? Why? How long did he prophesy? Did he write any book of history? Was he a faithful preacher?

5. How many chapters in the book called by Isaiah's name? Were all these written by him? How many must we leave out? Why? [Because they contain things that do not belong to his time.] Can you describe the vision of chapter vi.? How do we determine the date of any particular chapter? [By noting the historical allusions.] What history helps very much in this? [The Assyrian.]

6. What did Isaiah expect for his people? Were these hopes ever literally fulfilled? In what sense have they been fulfilled? Did Isaiah say that the knowledge of God should fill the earth? [Chap. xi. 9.] Is this now nearly true? Did Isaiah look for a righteous king? Has Jesus of Nazareth founded a kingdom? What is its nature?

LESSON XIII.

THE REFORM OF JOSIAH.

1. Partial Character of Hezekiah's Reform. — In the Lesson before the last we saw that King Hezekiah, probably under the influence of the prophet Isaiah, tried to better the national worship of Judah by destroying the idols all over the land. The effect of this procedure was to direct men's minds to Jerusalem as the centre of worship for the whole nation. True, the people were attached to the old shrines, which were more or less idolatrous; but in those troublous times, when powerful enemies were threatening the land, and Jerusalem was the only safe place, it was easier for the reform party to put down the local sanctuaries, and insist on the worship of Yahwe, whose great temple was in the national capital. We must not suppose, however, that Hezekiah's reform was spiritual, like Luther's; it did not attempt to teach men that God was to be worshipped in spirit and in truth (though Isaiah did insist on this), but only to abolish the worship of foreign deities. And even in this outward respect it was not thorough ; we learn from 2 Kings xxiii. 13, that it was not Hezekiah but Josiah who destroyed the shrines that Solomon had long before built to Ashtoreth, Chemosh, and Milcom.

2. The Reaction under Manasseh. — Moreover, it appears that what was done was the work of a reform party rather than a movement of the nation. The prophets, with Isaiah at their head, prevailed on the king to take vigorous measures against the idols, but it was not so easy to bring the people to give up the forms of worship that they had inherited from their fathers. And so, when Hezekiah died, about B.C. 607, his son and successor, Manasseh, set about restoring the former condition of things (2 Kings xxi.). He rebuilt the high places which his father had destroyed, re-established the Canaanitish worship of Baal and the Ashera images, together with magic arts and human sacrifices ; and further, in addition to Ahaz's sun-worship (2 Kings xxiii. 11, 12), he introduced the fuller worship of the hosts of heaven (sun, moon, and stars). He did not do all this without opposition. The Yahwe party withstood him with all their might. We do not know whether Isaiah was still alive (there is a late story that he was sawn asunder by Manasseh), but his disciples (Is. viii. 16), the prophets and others, no doubt tried to continue his work. The king was not a mild-natured man, and could not brook opposition ; he put to death those who stood in his way. The blood of the Yahwe party flowed freely in Jerusalem. Not that he refused to serve the God of Israel ; but he chose to serve other gods as well ; and the people doubtless approved his course. So it went on throughout his long reign of fifty-five years. The book of Chronicles says, indeed (2 Chron. xxxiii.), that he repented and destroyed the idols ; but this does not agree with the succeeding history as given in the book of Kings (compare 2 Kings xxiii. 12, with 2 Chron. xxxiii. 15). His son and successor, Amon, followed his father's example.

3. Progress of the Yahwe Party. — It might thus seem as if Manasseh had destroyed all that Isaiah and Hezekiah had with so much labor built up; the people had gone back to idols. But this was not the case. The party that favored the sole worship of Yahwe was not dead, and subsequent events show that it was gathering force. Hezekiah had begun to concentrate the national worship at Jerusalem, and pious men now saw that this was a necessity for the people. Hitherto the prophets generally had not disapproved of local shrines away from Jerusalem, provided they were devoted to Yahwe. But now, during and after Hezekiah's reign, they began to say that the people could never be weaned from other gods so long as they were allowed to worship wherever they pleased in the land; they must be required to go up to Jerusalem and offer their sacrifices in the temple of Yahwe there, and then they would get into the habit of worshipping Yahwe alone.

4. **The Book of Deuteronomy.** — After a while some prophetic man, whose name we do not know, compiled a law book, in which he laid it down as a rule that offerings must be made only in Jerusalem. As this rule was believed to be necessary to the true religious life of the nation, to be part of the law of Yahwe, it was naturally represented as having been given by the great prophet and lawgiver, Moses; in those days it was the custom to refer wisdom and authority to ancient sages. The book thus prepared was the one that we call Deuteronomy. Its legal part is contained in chapters xii.-xxvi.; this includes some older laws, together with customs which had been introduced during and after Hezekiah's time. The law of the one sanctuary is given in chapter xii.; see especially verses 5 and 13. To this legal portion is prefixed a general exhortation (put into the mouth of Moses) to be faithful to Yahwe (chapters i.-xii.); and at the end follow blessings and curses (xxvii.-xxx.), then a song (xxxii.), and a blessing of the tribes (xxxiii.) (poems probably composed at an earlier time), and some historical statements (xxxi. and xxxiv.). This earliest of the great law books of Israel is very interesting to us. It is the monument of a great religious conflict, and the sign of a great religious progress. It was the beginning of the movement that produced the Pentateuchal legislation. And it is full of deep

and pure religious feeling. It is abundantly quoted in the New Testament, for example in Matt. iv. 4, 7, 10.

5. Reform under Josiah. — We return now to the history of Judah. After Amon came the young Josiah, a boy eight years old, who for eighteen years let things go on as his father and grandfather had conducted them. But in the eighteenth year of his reign he was suddenly waked up by a curious event, namely, the finding of a law book in the temple. The king was engaged in repairing the temple (2 Kings xxii.), and, while the work was in progress, the priest Hilkiah reported that he had found a book of the law. The young king directed it to be read to him. He listened with astonishment and terror to the punishment denounced against idolatry. He saw that he and his people were acting contrary to the law as given in this book. How should they escape? He consulted the prophets and priests, and immediately set to work to extirpate idolatry. He undid all that his grandfather Manasseh had done; he made a clean sweep of idol-temples and images from Solomon's down. Read the graphic account in 2 Kings xxiii. It was very nearly the destruction of idolatry in Judah; after this we hear little of it. And the book that was read to Josiah was substantially the book of Deuteronomy.

LITERATURE.

1. On the history: the "Bible for Learners;" the histories of Kuenen, Wellhausen, and others above mentioned; J. H. Allen, "Hebrew Men and Times," Boston, 1879.

2. On Deuteronomy: Introduction of Bleek-Wellhausen; W. R. Smith's "Old Testament in the Jewish Church."

QUESTIONS.

1. What had Hezekiah tried to do? What was the effect of this? Were the people attached to the old shrines? Why was it easier at this time to turn the worship to Jerusalem? Was Hezekiah's reform spiritual? What did it do? Was it thorough even in this respect?

2. Was the whole nation concerned in this movement of Hezekiah? What happened when he died? What did Manasseh do? Who opposed

him? How did he treat them? Was he also a worshipper of Yahwe? What does the book of Chronicles say of him? Is this probable?

3. Had Manasseh destroyed the party that favored the sole worship of Yahwe? What had Hezekiah begun to do? What did pious men now see? Had the prophets hitherto condemned the local shrines devoted to Yahwe? What change took place in their views during and after Hezekiah's time?

4. What book was written about this time? What rule did it lay down? To what ancient prophet was it ascribed? Can you turn to this book and point out its divisions? Why is it interesting to us? Where is it quoted in the New Testament? What is the date of its composition? [Probably not far from B.C. 622.]

5. What king succeeded Manasseh and Amon? How old was he when he came to the throne? How long did things go on in the old way? What roused him? How did this happen? What did Josiah do? What was the book that was found in the temple?

LESSON XIV.

JEREMIAH AND THE FALL OF JERUSALEM.

1. The Capture of Jerusalem by the Chaldeans. — We must now briefly relate the events that led to the destruction of Jerusalem, and the temporary breaking up of the nation of Judah; they are described in the books of Kings and Chronicles, and of the last years there is a vivid picture in the book of Jeremiah. After the death of Hezekiah the land had rest for many years. It was subject to Assyria, but the Assyrians, occupied elsewhere, made no new invasion. The surrounding petty nations, the Moabites, Ammonites, and Philistines, gave, as it seems, no serious trouble, though there were, perhaps, incursions by the Arabs. Manasseh, Amon, and Josiah devoted themselves wholly to internal affairs. But great changes in the history of the world were impending, in which the little kingdom of Judah was to be involved. About B.C. 606 (the date is uncertain) the Assyrian empire fell before the combined attack of the Medes and Babylonians, and in the partition of territory that followed, Judah, with the rest of

Canaan, was assigned to Babylon. The end came soon. About
B.C. 609 the king of Egypt had made an expedition against the
Assyrians; Josiah, king of Judah, opposed his advance, and
was defeated and slain at Megiddo (2 Kings xxiii. 29, 30). The
king of Egypt deposed Josiah's son, Jehoahaz, who had succeeded his father, and set up in his place another son of Josiah,
Jehoiakim, as his vassal-king. But the power of the Egyptian
empire was speedily broken. In B.C. 605 King Necho was
defeated at Karkemish by Nebuchadnezzar, the young king of
Babylon, and after this the king of Egypt was shut up in his
own land (2 Kings xxiv. 7). Jehoiakim submitted to Nebuchadnezzar, and, though he rebelled, remained the vassal of Babylon. After reigning eleven years he died and was succeeded
by his son Jehoiachin, who at the end of three months was
carried, together with many of his subjects, to Babylon by the
Chaldeans (that is, the Babylonians); here he remained a pris-
oner thirty-seven years, and was then released by Nebuchadnezzar's son and successor, Avilmarduk (2 Kings xxv. 27-30). In
his stead the Chaldeans placed on the throne of Jerusalem
Zedekiah (B.C. 598), a weak prince, who angered Nebuchadnezzar by various attempts at rebellion. Finally, about B.C. 587,
the latter came up to Jerusalem, besieged and captured it,
destroyed the temple, and carried off the greater part of the
people to Babylon. This was the end of the Davidic kingdom
of Judah, which had existed (from Rehoboam's accession)
nearly four hundred years. Presently we shall see a new community established in Judah, and then another kingdom (the
Hasmonean), and then will come Christianity. All through
these years God is preparing the Jews for the coming of the
Christ. Though the nation was broken up and held in subjec-
tion by foreigners, it continued to learn new truths of religion.
For a description of the last days of the Judah kingdom, see
Jer. xxxvii.-xliii.

2. Nahum, Zephaniah, and Habakkuk. — The prophets
who flourished in the seventh century B.C. are Nahum, Zephaniah, Habakkuk, and Jeremiah. To the three first of these we
need give only a word. Nahum (perhaps about B.C. 630) directs

his prophecy against the Assyrian empire (Nineveh), of which he describes the oppression and predicts the downfall; the Assyrians had been cruel to Judah, and Yahwe would destroy them. The prophecy was probably uttered about the time when the Assyrian power began to wane and enemies gathered around Nineveh. Zephaniah's prophecy falls not far from Nahum's, but its exact date is not determined. His view embraces almost all the surrounding nations, — Assyria, Ethiopia, the Philistines, Moab, and Ammon. He speaks of an approaching "day of Yahwe" (i. 14), when idolatry should be rooted out, Judah's enemies destroyed, and Judah itself dwell in safety; and he rebukes those who thought that Yahwe sat with folded hands, and had nothing to do with the affairs of the nation (i. 12). Habakkuk, writing somewhere about B.C. 605, announces the speedy coming of the Chaldeans, their might and victory, and their following overthrow; his refrain and the ground of his hope is: "Yahwe is in his holy temple; let all the earth keep silence before him" (ii. 20). There is added a beautiful hymn (iii.) in which God's majesty is celebrated.

3. Jeremiah's Life. — More space must be given to Jeremiah, one of the most important of the prophets of Israel, a man of intense patriotism, deep spirituality, and lofty faith in the mercy and power of Israel's God. Thanks to the biographical details in his book, we know more of his personal character and fortunes than of those of any other prophet. In some points he resembles the Apostle Paul: like him he is intense in feeling, and eager and unwearied in action, and like him he is condemned to be misunderstood and hated by his countrymen. On the other hand, unlike Paul, he was retiring by nature, shrinking from a public career, yet driven by an inward voice to a life of ceaseless conflict. According to the superscription of his book he began to prophesy in the thirteenth year of Josiah's reign, about B.C. 626. He denounced the wickedness, the idolatry, and the religious formality of the people; Yahwe, said he (vii. 22, 23), has commanded not offerings of animals, but obedience to his will. On one occasion (vii. 2) he stood in the gate of the temple, and told the throng of worshippers that this house was nothing unless they amended their ways. Later, in the fourth year of Jehoiakim (B.C. 605), the prophet's secretary, Baruch, wrote his words down, and they were read before the king, who showed his appreciation of them by cutting the book to pieces with his knife and throwing it into the fire (xxxvi.). In fact, the political and religious ideas of Jeremiah were very different from those of the king and princes. They were for resisting the Babylonians and asserting their independence; he saw that this was fatal folly, — they could not stand against the mighty power of Babylon. They accused him of treason (this was when Zedekiah was king), and threw him into a dungeon, whence he was released only when Jerusalem was taken (xxxvii., xxxviii.). He was not carried to Babylon (xxxix.), but after a while was forced by a party of Jews to go with them to Egypt (xlii., xliii.), where he probably died (the date of his death is unknown).

4. His Faith and Teaching. — Jeremiah trusted wholly to the truthfulness and goodness of the God of Israel, and his hopes were fulfilled, though not in the way that he expected. He supposed that the people would go into captivity (xxv. 8-11), and that afterwards their deliverance would be effected through a king, a descendant of David, who should be called "Yahwe our righteousness" (xxiii. 5, 6), that is, he should be a man who should show forth in his life and government the righteousness of which Yahwe would approve (the same name is given to Judah, xxxiii. 16). No such king came; but the captivity itself taught Israel something about true righteousness, and long afterwards God sent Jesus with a more perfect teaching. The prophet said also that the time was coming when God's law should be written on the people's heart; when they should obey him freely and gladly (xxxi. 31-34); and this is the spirit of the New Testament.

5. His Book. — Jeremiah's prophecies were gathered and written at various times, and they are not arranged in chronological order in the Hebrew and our English version (the order is better in the Greek version). The date of each prophecy must be made out by the superscriptions and the contents. A few passages now included in the book were not written by Jeremiah: chapters l., li., belong to the time of the Exile (like Is. xiii., xiv); the prophecy against Moab (xlviii.) appears to be an imitation of Is. xv., xvi., but, if this is so, it may nevertheless be Jeremiah's.

LITERATURE.

1. On Nahum: the general works on prophecy above mentioned; the "Speaker's Commentary," and the "Kurzgefasstes Exegetisches Handbuch;" articles in Schenkel's Bibel-Lexicon and Encyclopædia Britannica.

2. On Zephaniah: the same as for Nahum, and articles in Herzog's Encyclopädie and Encyclopædia Britannica.

3. On Habakkuk: the same.

4. On Jeremiah: the same as above, and Lange's Commentary.

QUESTIONS.

1. Where is the destruction of Jerusalem described? What was the state of Judah under Kings Manasseh, Amon, and Josiah? What nations overthrew the Assyrian empire? To whose share did Judah fall? How was Josiah killed? Whom did the Egyptian king place on the throne of Jerusalem? By whom was the power of Egypt broken? Who succeeded Jehoiakim as king? What became of him? What was the character of Zedekiah? By whom was Jerusalem captured? When? How long had the Davidic kingdom of Judah lasted? For what was God preparing the Jews?

2. What four prophets flourished in the seventh century? Can you turn to their writings in the Bible? Of what does Nahum speak? What nations does Zephaniah's view embrace? Of what day does he speak? Whom does he rebuke? What event does Habakkuk announce? What, then, is his probable date? What sentence expresses his hope?

3. What was Jeremiah's character? Why do we know more of him than of the other prophets? Wherein does he resemble the Apostle Paul? In what is he unlike Paul? When did he begin to prophesy? What did he denounce? What did he tell the worshippers at the gate of the temple? Who wrote his words down? To whom were they read? What did the king do? Were the prophecies written down again? [Yes, with additions; see Jer. xxxvi. 32.] How did Jeremiah's political and religious ideas differ

from those of the king and princes? Of what did they accuse him? What became of him?

4. To what did Jeremiah trust? Were his hopes fulfilled? What did he expect? Did such a king arise? What did the captivity teach Israel? Where did the prophet say God's law should be written? Is this the spirit of the New Testament?

5. When were Jeremiah's prophecies written down? Are they arranged in chronological order in the English version? In what version is the order better? Where and when was the Greek version made? [In Alexandria in Egypt, about B.C. 200.] How do we make out the dates of the prophecies? What is to be said of the authorship of chapters l., li.? Why do we suppose that they were not written by Jeremiah? [Because they say that the people are already in captivity in Babylon, and because they are hostile to Babylon, while Jeremiah is always friendly to that kingdom, which he regards as Yahwe's instrument for chastising Israel.]

LESSON XV.

THE EXILE.

1. The Carrying Away of the Jews to Babylon. — When we speak of "the Exile," we commonly mean the captivity of the Jews in Babylon from the capture and destruction of the city of Jerusalem (B.C. 587) to the return of a portion of the people to Palestine (B.C. 537 or 536). A large part of the northern kingdom, Israel, had been carried away to Assyria some time before this (B.C. 720), but some of them had remained, and with the Assyrian settlers formed the mixed people called Samaritans (see Lesson XI.); this captivity is called the Exile of the Ten Tribes, or the Assyrian Exile. The Babylonian Exile, of which we have now to speak, was more important than the Assyrian captivity for the political and religious fortunes of the nation, and therefore is usually called "the Exile." King Nebuchadnezzar (or, as the name is more properly written, Nebuchadrezzar) carried off first a large body of people on the accession of Jehoiachin (B.C. 598), and then another large body when he took the city, eleven years later (2 Kings xxiv. 14–16,

xxv. 11). There remained in Judah only the poorer class of husbandmen, or tillers of the soil, and vinedressers (xxv. 12). Over these the Babylonian general appointed a Judean as governor; but some fanatics, who still fancied they might be independent of Babylon, assassinated him, and the people, fearing the vengeance of the Babylonians, left their country and went down to Egypt (2 Kings xxv. 22-26, Jer. xxxix.-xliii.). Others of the people had probably fled to the surrounding territory of Moab and Ammon and Philistia; and so Judea was left desolate, almost uninhabited, till the return ordered by Cyrus (see next Lesson). The nation is no longer in Canaan, but in Babylon, and thither we must follow it.

2. The Results of the Exile.— The prophet Jeremiah had declared (Jer. xxv. 11) that Judah and all the nations round about should be carried off, and should serve the king of Babylon seventy years, which is to be taken as a round number; what became of the other nations we do not know, but the captivity of Judah lasted fifty years if we reckon from the destruction of the city (B.C. 587-537), sixty years from the accession and carrying off of Jehoiachin (598-537, see Ezek. i. 2), and about seventy years from the fourth year of Jehoiakim (605-537, see Jer. xxv. 1, 11). The time is of little consequence; we are more concerned with what the captive Jews learned in Babylon. Their political independence was destroyed, and they did not regain it till shortly before the birth of Christ. As to their religious ideas, these four things may be said: 1. The Exile brought them on a great way toward religious manhood. It did this in part by sifting them, putting the best people together, and casting off the rest. When the Israelites first settled in Canaan, they all worshipped a number of gods, and were like children in their religious ideas and practices; they were not at all different from their neighbors. Gradually the more enlightened among them came to see that it was better for them to worship only their own god, Yahwe, and they thought of him as not only powerful but also holy and just. Then men like Amos said that Yahwe, though he was the God of Israel, was also the ruler of all the nations. Finally, in the Exile, the deepest thinkers came to the conclusion that the idols of the other nations were nothing, and that there was only one God in the world, and he was Israel's holy God. When they had once got hold of this idea, they never lost it; after this, idolatry could not tempt them, for they despised it. God was bringing them on by a sure path to know him. Perhaps the more enlightened and spiritual of the Jews would have reached this faith in the one God (monotheism) even if they had stayed in their own land; but the chastisement of exile made them more thoughtful, and at the same time, by breaking up the government, brought the better people together into a society or church, and in this way hastened the result. 2. The Exile not only destroyed idolatry among the Judean captives, but also gave them larger and more spiritual views of Yahwe's relation to his people. They had thought that the temple at Jerusalem was his dwelling-place. Now the temple was destroyed, there were no sacrifices, they had to worship without priests and offerings. The earthly kingdom was destroyed, and Yahwe alone was king. Israel was the servant of foreign nations, but Israel had something better than military power, — it had the presence of the true God, and his instruction; and it should become a light to the other nations to guide them to God. Israel was suffering, but by its suffering should atone for sin and reconcile men to God. So taught some of the prophets (Is. xlix. 6, liii. 11, 12). This was a great progress in spirituality. 3. Another result was that the Jews now began to arrange their religious law. There had been several collections of political and religious rules of life. One of these, the oldest of which we know, compiled, perhaps, about b.c. 800, is contained in Ex. xxi.–xxiii. Another one is the book of Deuteronomy, of which we spoke in Lesson XIII. There was an increasing interest in this subject, and the interest was probably further heightened by acquaintance with the religious organization of the Babylonians, which was more perfect than that of the Israelites. The prophet Ezekiel drew up a new code. Other men were, no doubt, thinking how to better the temple-service when it should be restored. Then they all began to feel that a clear moral and religious law was necessary in order that the people might lead a worthy life.

We shall see how this thought afterwards bore fruit, and prepared the world for the coming of the Christ. 4. It seems also that the Jews learned at this time from the Babylonians a number of stories about the creation and early times of the world; and, after purging them of heathen notions, included them in their sacred books. They are now found in Gen. i.–xi. As we read nothing of these in the books of the Old Testament written before the Exile, it seems probable that the Jews now, for the first time, came to a distinct knowledge of them.

3. Historical Books written at this Time. — During the Exile, several books of the Old Testament were written. History proper is among the latest products of a national literature, and among the Jews it seems not to have flourished till about this time. There had before been annals and short narratives of particular periods; now, when the nation was broken up, in the quiet of exile, or in the desolation of Canaan, men began to think over the past, and wish to give an historical explanation of it. It was probably now that the books of Judges, Ruth, Samuel, and Kings were written. On these, see Lessons V., VI., VII. The book of Kings takes the same general view of religious law as Deuteronomy; it blames all those who sacrificed elsewhere than at Jerusalem. Judges and Samuel do not insist on this rule; they are more largely made up of popular stories, and may have been composed earlier, perhaps about B.C. 650. The book of Ruth is a charming story of an ancestress of David. Perhaps other historical books were written just before and during the Exile; but these are all that have come down to us.

4. Obadiah and Lamentations. — Some prophetical books belong to this period. From Obadiah (otherwise unknown to us) we have a word against the Edomites (perhaps directly after the destruction of Jerusalem), who, as it appears from the prophecy (verses 10–14), had helped to plunder the city and cut off the fugitives. About this time was composed the pathetic little poem (or rather, collection of five poems) called "Lamentations," a lament over the fallen city. Our English version ascribes it to Jeremiah, but the Hebrew does not.

Two other prophets we must reserve for another Lesson.

LITERATURE.

1. The commentaries on Ruth are the same as those on Judges, Obadiah goes along with the rest of the Minor Prophets, and Lamentations with Jeremiah.

QUESTIONS.

1. What do we commonly mean when we speak of "the Exile"? What is the Assyrian Exile? By what other name is it called? Who were the Samaritans? In what respect is the Babylonian Exile more important? On what two occasions did Nebuchadnezzar carry off the Jews to Babylon? What people were left in Judea? What became of them? What was the state of the land? Where was the nation of Judah now?

2. How long did Jeremiah declare the Jews should remain captives in Babylon? Can we make out this number exactly? Is it of much consequence? What is of more consequence? What had become of the nation's political independence? What was the first effect of the Exile on the religious condition of Israel? How did it sift the people? What was the worship of the Israelites when they first settled in Canaan? What did the more enlightened (the prophets, for example) gradually come to see? Afterwards, what did men like Amos say? Finally, to what conclusion did the deepest thinkers come? Would they have reached this conclusion without the Exile? How did the Exile help? What is monotheism? What was the second result of the Exile? What did Israel have that was better than military power? How could Israel, though in servitude to other nations, be a light to them? Did one of the prophets think that Israel's suffering would aid others? Can you turn to the passage? What was the third result of the Exile? What collections of laws were there before this period? Was there now an increase of interest on this subject? What prophet drew up a new code? [See Ezek. xl.-xlviii., especially xliii.-xlvi.] What did men begin to feel? Fourthly, what stories did the Jews probably learn at this time? From whom? Where are they found in the Bible?

3. Is history among the latest products of a national literature? Can you tell why? What historical books were probably written about this time? Had there been earlier historical writings? Of what character? Wherein does the book of Kings agree with Deuteronomy? How are Judges and Samuel largely made up? Can you turn to these books, and point out some of the stories? What is the book of Ruth? Can you repeat the story of Ruth?

4. Against whom is the prophecy of Obadiah directed? What had they done? What is the subject of the book called Lamentations? Was it written by Jeremiah? [Hardly; it says, for example (ii. 9), that Judah's prophets find no vision from Yahwe.]

LESSON XVI.
THE PROPHETS OF THE EXILE.

1. Condition of the Exiles. — The best part of the people of Israel had been carried off to Assyria and Babylonia. Some of them (especially of those first carried away, B C. 720) were no doubt absorbed in the Assyrian population; the later captives (the Judeans) formed a colony which maintained itself separate from the surrounding people. There is no reason to suppose that they suffered in body, at least in the early part of their captivity. Doubtless they would sometimes think of native land and homes, and their hearts would grow sick with longing (Ps. cxxxvii. 1); but in general the most of them were comfortable. It was as if they had all migrated to this distant land (whence their forefathers had long ago come). Their conquerors, the Babylonians, were not unkind to them. They seem to have had a district of their own, where they built houses, and planted, and reaped, and managed their own affairs; and the prophet Jeremiah exhorted them to be obedient and friendly to the people among whom they lived (Jer. xxix. 5-7). Indeed, he believed that the hope of the nation lay in these captives, whom God was purifying by this chastisement. Not that they all became righteous and devoted to God. There was discontent, murmuring, oppression, and probably idolatry among them. Towards the end of the Exile, possibly, the hand of their masters pressed heavily on them (Isa. lii., liii.). But by all their experiences the better part of the people were learning of God's ways; and we shall find out something of their religious ideas from the two great prophets, Ezekiel and him who is commonly called the Second Isaiah.

2. Ezekiel. — Our only source of information about Ezekiel is his book; please turn as often as possible to the references, and see for yourselves what he says. 1. Ezekiel seems to have been carried off to Mesopotamia at the same time with King Jehoiachin (B.C. 598) (Ezek. i. 1, 2 Kings xxiv. 15), and to have lived there the rest of his life in a place called Tel-Abib, by the river or canal Kebar (Ezek. iii. 15). He began to prophesy B.C. 593. He was a priest (i. 3), and though there was no temple of Yahwe in Babylon, and he could not offer sacrifices, he was very much interested in the ritual, as we shall see; in this he was unlike Jeremiah, who, though a priest, cared little for sacrifices. He was married (xxiv. 18), and seems to have lived comfortably in his own house (Jeremiah was unmarried). He was friendly to the Babylonians, and probably mixed with them and studied their religious customs. He was a bold and resolute man; his style of writing is not highly imaginative, but is striking by his free use of bold imagery. 2. His book may be divided as follows: first come reproofs and threatenings directed against Israel, all dated before the destruction of Jerusalem (i.–xxiv.); then prophecies against foreign nations (xxv.–xxxii.); a word when the city was taken (xxxiii.), followed by prophecies of comfort to Israel, and a word against Seir or Edom (xxxiv.–xxxix.); finally, a great vision of the restored Israel, an account of the temple and worship when the people should go back to Canaan (xl.–xlviii.). 3. Ezekiel believed that the captivity was ordered by God, that he might purify his people, and show forth his power to the other nations (xxxvii. 27, 28). He expected that Israel would be restored as a nation to Canaan, that a king of the line of David would reign over them as in former times (xxxvii. 21–26), that the temple would be rebuilt in greater splendor than before, and that the people would dwell in their land forever. They did indeed go back to Canaan, but not just as he expected; God's plans were not exactly those of the prophet. 4. Expecting his people's return to their land, he drew up a constitution or religious code for that happy time. He wrote this in the form of a vision; it is contained in chapters xl.–xlviii. It was never carried into effect, for, when the people did return to Canaan, they were too poor and weak to adopt his magnificent plans. From the rules and laws that he gives it appears that he was not acquainted with the code of Numbers and Leviticus; this was drawn up later. But he goes beyond the code of Deuteronomy. 5. Ezekiel's ethical code is lofty and clear. He felt deeply his own responsibility as a religious teacher (iii., xxxiii.). He insisted strongly on every man's personal responsibility (xviii.); he who does wrong, said he, must answer for it himself. He was a firm believer in the holiness and justice of the God of Israel, and a faithful teacher of his people. He was a priest, and perhaps thought overmuch of the temple and sacrifices. But these were really necessary at that time, and he was truly a God-fearing man, filled with the spirit of God.

3. The Second Isaiah. — Ezekiel wrote in the early part of the captivity, when Israel's part was to submit to the Babylonians. After a while the Medes and Persians began to be powerful, and the Israelites hoped to be delivered by them, and restored to their own land. Then the prophets began to speak against the Babylonians. Toward the end of the Exile there lived a great prophet, whose name we do not know. It happened somehow that his writings were joined on to those of Isaiah, whom we have already studied (Lesson XII.), and they are now printed in our Bible as chapters xl.-lxvi. of the prophecy of Isaiah. For want of a better name we call him the Second Isaiah (it is possible that his name was really Isaiah, and that this was the reason of his being confounded with the earlier prophet). The later Jews thought he was the same as the Isaiah of Hezekiah's time; but we know from his writings that he lived in the latter part of the Exile. About him we may say: 1. His style is marked by loftiness of imagination; more than any other prophet he maintains his thought in the region of the poetic and the ideal. 2. He looks to the speedy restoration of his people to their own land. He speaks of the great Persian king, Cyrus, as having already conquered many nations, and as now approaching Babylon, and calls him "righteous," and Yahwe's "shepherd," and "anointed one" (xli. 2, xliv. 28, xlv. 1-4); by him the Chaldeans (Babylonians) shall be destroyed, and Israel sent back to worship Yahwe in Jerusalem (xlvii. 1, lii. 1-12). 3. He has little to say about temple and sacrifices. He rather describes Israel as the "servant of Yahwe," chastened by captivity that it may more perfectly perform the divine will in enlightening and saving the other nations. See xli. 8, xlii. 1-4, 19, xliv. 1-8, xlix. 1-3. In one or two places he speaks of the pious of Israel as atoning by their suffering for the sins of their own people and of other nations;

so in xlix. 6 and the section from lii. 13 to the end of liii. This last passage, particularly chapter liii., is a beautiful description of an innocent person suffering for others. The prophet is speaking of the pious people of Israel, the spiritual kernel of the nation; but it is true of all God's servants, and particularly of Jesus, to whom it is applied in the New Testament (Acts viii. 32, 33). He was in a special sense the "servant of the Lord" (see Luke iv. 17–21). 4. It is hard to give an outline of the prophet's thought. His book is one continued strain (with here and there a slight exception) of splendid portraiture of Israel's coming glory through its knowledge of Yahwe. He ridicules idolatry (xl. 18–20, xliv. 9–20; and compare Ps. cxv. 4–8), but he has nothing to say against any foreign nation but Babylon.

4. Other Exilian Writings. — About this time also were probably written the following prophecies: Is. xiii., xiv. 1–27, xxxiv., xxxv., Jer. l., li.; and several of the Psalms, such as xiv. (and liii., which is the same thing), cxxx., cxxxvii., and perhaps li.

LITERATURE.

1. On the Exile in general: the histories of Israel, and particularly Ewald's.

2. On Ezekiel: articles in encyclopædias and commentaries, particularly Smend's (in the "Kurzgefasstes Exegetisches Handbuch").

3. On Isaiah II.: Ewald's "Prophets," commentaries of Knobel and Cheyne; article in Encycl. Brit.; Matthew Arnold has printed an excellent little edition of the prophecy, with brief notes, London, 1872.

QUESTIONS.

1. What became of the first Israelitish captives in Assyria? — what of the later Judean captives in Babylon? Did they suffer? Were their conquerors unkind to them? Did they make homes for themselves in Babylon? What advice did Jeremiah give them? What did he believe in reference to them? Were they all good? From what source shall we learn something of their religious ideas?

2. What is our source of information about Ezekiel? When was he carried away to Mesopotamia? When did he begin to prophesy? What was his calling in life? Wherein was he like and wherein unlike Jeremiah? How did he feel toward the Babylonians? What was his character? — his style? Can you turn to his book and point out its divisions by chapters? What did he think was the object of the captivity? What did he expect for his people? Did this come to pass exactly according to his ideas? What did he draw up for the people? Did they adopt it when they returned to Canaan? Why not? Is his ritual as full as that of Leviticus and Numbers? Is it fuller than that of Deuteronomy? What is the character of his ethical code? How did he feel for himself? What did he insist on? Was he a faithful teacher and prophet?

3. When did the prophets Ezekiel and Jeremiah speak kindly of the Babylonians? What change took place in the circumstances? How did the prophets then speak of Babylon? At what time did a great anonymous prophet arise? What happened to his writings? Where are they now printed? What do we call him? What did the later Jews think of him? What date for him do his writings indicate? What is his style? What did he look to for the people?. How does he speak of Cyrus? What does he call him? What does he expect him to do for Israel? Does he say much of temples and sacrifices? How does he describe Israel? What does he say of atoning by suffering? What chapter speaks especially of this? Is this true of all true servants of God? Of whom is it particularly true? Is it easy to give an outline of the thought of the whole prophesy? How does it speak of idolatry? May we suppose that Ezekiel and the Second Isaiah represent different sides of the ideas of the Jewish captives? Can you tell what the more pious and spiritual among them hoped for? [See what is said in the Lesson of the hopes of the two prophets.]

4. What other prophecies were probably written during the Exile? What Psalms? Why do we suppose that these were composed in Exile? [Because they contain references and allusions to the Exile.]

LESSON XVII.

HISTORY AND PROPHETIC WRITINGS UP TO THE TIME OF THE MACCABEES.

1. Character of the Period. — We have now reached the priestly period of the history of the Israelitish religion. The great prophets had done their work; they had preached righteousness of life and spirituality of worship. Through the guidance of God Israel had thrown off idolatry, and now, when the Exile was over, had come to worship one God. But now also, just in proportion as they honored their God, they began to wish for stricter rules of outward religious service. They felt that they must keep themselves separate from the other nations, who worshipped idols; and to do this they must build around themselves a hedge of laws and ceremonies. This sort of service would of course be directed by priests. A few prophets spoke after the Exile; but the priests gradually got the control of things. It is this religious progress that we are most concerned with, from the return from exile to the time of the Maccabees; the political history is meagre and of little interest.

2. **The Return from Exile.** — In the year B.C. 539 Babylon was taken and the Babylonian empire destroyed by the Medes and Persians under Cyrus. The new empire thus established by the Persians comprised the whole of western Asia, and Judea was one of its provinces. The Persian king was not unwilling to have a people friendly to him dwelling on the border of his empire towards Egypt; so he gave permission to the Jewish captives in Babylon to go back to their own land, and some of them accordingly went (B.C. 536). Not all of the people returned; perhaps the majority stayed in Babylon, not choosing to risk the chances of the desolate and defenceless land of Judah, and in Babylon their descendants dwelt for more than a thousand years. About 40,000 (with 7,000 servants) returned to Canaan, under the lead of Zerubbabel (Ezra i., ii. 64), and of these over 4,000 were priests. Very few Levites came. Till a short while before, all Levites had been priests (so it is in the book of Deuteronomy), but about Ezekiel's time a distinction was made between them; the Levites were not permitted to offer sacrifices, and were in an inferior position. Hence not many of them cared to go back to Canaan, where they could not expect positions of honor.

3. **The Building of the Temple.** — We can easily understand that the returned exiles were kept busy building their

houses, sowing their fields, and bringing their little community into shape. However, they did not forget the claims of religion; soon after their return they set up the altar, and laid the foundations of the temple. But there were various hinderances : the people, hard pressed to get their daily bread (Hag. i. 6), were probably slack in work; and it seems that their jealous neighbors made trouble for them at the Persian court (Ezra iv. 24). For about sixteen years nothing was done. Then (B.C. 520) the prophets Haggai and Zechariah came forward with exhortations, the people set to work, and the new temple (called the second temple) was finished in the sixth year of Darius Hystaspis, B.C. 515. It was not as grand as Ezekiel's, nor as splendid as Solomon's; when the foundations were laid, the old men, remembering the glory of the first house of Yahwe, wept in the midst of their rejoicing, seeing how much less was the outward glory of this second house (Ezra iii. 12, 13). But Haggai told them afterwards that the glory of the latter house should be greater than that of the former (Hag. ii. 9); and so it turned out. This handful of people had founded the new Jewish Church.

4. Haggai and Zechariah. — Two prophets belong to this period. Of the first, Haggai, a few words have been preserved, spoken in the second year of Darius, B C. 520. They are exhortations to build the temple, and promises of blessing. He seems to have expected political power for his people (ii. 20-23); but God had other designs. The second prophet, Zechariah, had a number of visions (B.C. 520), encouraging the people to build the temple, and again (B.C. 518), taught them that they were not to fast in commemoration of the capture of the city (chapter vii.), but to be righteous in their lives, and hope for God's blessing (viii.). Only chapters i.-viii. of this book are the production of this prophet, the contemporary of Haggai; chapters ix.-xiv. belong to a different time.

5. The History up to the Maccabees. — After the building of the temple, the Jews in Canaan seem to have gone on quietly for a number of years, under Persian governors; we have no account of this period. But their religion moved steadily forward. Those Jews who had stayed in Babylonia had been studying the law, and about B.C. 457 one of them, named Ezra, came over to Judea and introduced or gave a great impulse to this study among the people. His efforts were seconded by Nehemiah, who about B.C. 444 was sent over by the Persian king to be governor. Nehemiah also built the walls of Jerusalem, and decidedly strengthened the feeble little nation. See the interesting account of all this in his book, and in Ezra vii.-x. After this the Jewish political history is a blank for almost 300 years; there are no reliable records relating to it. Judea remained a province of the Persian empire till its overthrow by Alexander the Great (B.C. 332), and then came into the hands of the Greeks. For many years it was a bone of contention between the Greek kingdoms of Egypt and Syria, but finally came into the possession of the latter (B.C. 198). Then followed soon the Maccabean struggle (Lesson XX.). Meanwhile several important events had occurred. 1. Nearly the whole of Canaan, or, as it was afterwards called, Palestine, was filled up by Jews; and a good many foreigners likewise came to live in it. 2. On the other hand, the Jews began to settle in all the countries of the Greek and Roman world, where they became very prosperous. They were especially numerous and influential in Egypt. They even built a temple there, at a place called Leontopolis in Heliopolis, but this did not amount to much; all over the world the Jews remained faithful to the temple at Jerusalem. More important was the Greek translation of the Old Testament which the Alexandrian Jews began about B.C. 275 and finished about B.C. 100. This is what is now called the Septuagint; it is a great help in the study of the Old Testament. 3. The Samaritans (see Lesson XI.) gradually came to be a distinct religious community. They built a temple on Mount Gerizim (Deut. xxvii. 12), and kept up a worship of the one God independent of Jerusalem (John iv. 20). They also had a copy of the Pentateuch, the text of which has been preserved. 4. The Jews seem to have accepted certain religious ideas from the Persians, and to have developed certain of their own ideas under Persian influence. For example, the doctrine of angels becomes distincter in this period, and the idea of guardian angels, found in the books of Daniel and Tobit, is very much like that of the Persians. Possibly also it was under Persian influence that the doctrine of the resurrection of the body was acquired. 5. During this period synagogues were established (see Lesson XXIV.).

6. **Malachi, Joel, Zechariah II., Zechariah III.**— We can barely mention the prophets of this period. Malachi (about B.C. 420) may be called a legal prophet; he rebukes the people for their failure to fulfil the requirements of the temple-service. Joel probably lived early in the Greek period. On the occasion of a great plague of locusts (i.-ii. 27) he predicted the outpouring of God's spirit on all flesh (ii. 28-32; see Acts ii. 16-21), and announced a judgment of the nations (iii.). Not far from this time belongs the prophecy contained in Zech. xii.-xiv., which predicts the triumph of Yahwe's worship at Jerusalem. The date of Zech. ix.-xi. is uncertain, but it also seems to belong to the Greek period, perhaps about B.C. 300. It speaks of Israel's suffering and future restoration to prosperity. All these prophets taught that holiness of life, in obedience to God, and with faith in him, would bring blessing to the people; and the blessing did really come, not in the shape of political independence and power, but in the person of the Great Teacher whom God raised up out of Israel.

LITERATURE.

1. On the history: Ewald's "History of Israel;" Prideaux's "Connection;" Stanley's "Jewish Church," vol. iii.; Reuss, "Geschichte des Alten Testaments," Braunschweig, 1881.

2. On the Septuagint: the books of Introduction and the cyclopedias.

3. On the history of the doctrines of angels and the resurrection: Nicolas, "Doctrines Religieuses des Juifs;" articles in Herzog, Schenkel, Encyclopædia Britannica; histories of Ewald and others.

4. On the prophets: the commentaries on the Minor Prophets; articles in Encyclopædia Britannica. On Zech. ix.-xiv., Stade in the "Zeitschrift für Alttestamentliche Wissenschaft."

QUESTIONS.

1. What period have we now reached? What had the prophets preached? What had Israel done? What did they now wish? Why should they keep themselves separate from other nations? How could they do this? Who would have the control of this service? With what are we concerned in this period?

2. When and by whom was Babylon taken? What was the extent of the Persian empire? Why was the Persian king willing that the Jews should return to their land? When did they go back? Did all go? Why not? How many returned? How many of these were priests? Why did more priests than Levites return?

3. How were the returned exiles at first employed? Did they forget the claims of religion? What did they do? What hinderances were in their way? When did the two prophets come forward? When was the temple finished? Why did the old men weep? What did Haggai say? What had this handful of people founded?

4. When did Haggai prophesy? What does he say? What did he expect? What was the object of Zechariah's visions? What else did he teach? What part of the book called Zechariah belongs to this time?

5. After the building of the temple, what was the condition of the Jews? Did their religion go forward? What Jews had been studying the law? Who came to Judea? When? Whence? For what purpose? Who seconded his efforts? What did he do? What of the history for the next three hundred years? Into whose hands did Judea finally fall? Mention an important event that occurred during this period? Mention another? Where were the Jews especially numerous? What did they build? Did it amount to much? What translation did they make? When? What third event occurred? What did they build? What book had they? Under what influence do the Jews seem at this time to have attained new religious ideas? What doctrines now first clearly appear? What religious gatherings now came into use?

6. When did Joel probably live? Can you point out the divisions of his book? Who quotes him in the New Testament? Has God's spirit been poured out on all men? What is the date of Zech. xii.-xiv.? What does it predict? The date of Malachi? For what does he rebuke the people? Of what does Zech. ix.-xi. speak? Do we know its date certainly? What did all these prophets teach? How has the blessing come?

LESSON XVIII.

EZRA'S REFORM, AND THE PENTATEUCH.

We must go back, and look for a moment at the great religious movement which is connected with the name of Ezra. We shall have to ask what it is that he did, and how the Pentateuch came to have its present form. This is the starting-point of the Judaism of Christ's time.

1. Progress of Legal and Priestly Ideas. — It was a long time before the Israelites built up their great Law, which we now have in the Pentateuch. At first they got on without written law. Their judges and kings governed according to their own notions of right. The priests offered sacrifices all over the land according to customs that had been handed down from generation to generation. Gradually, as society became better organized, the religious laws or rules were more accurately defined, and the priests, who carried out these laws, became more and more influential. Small collections of laws were made by pious men. As the devotion to Yahwe, God of Israel, increased, the necessity for a formal worship according to rule was more deeply felt. This feeling was strengthened during the Exile, when the more thoughtful Israelites began to reflect on the condition of the nation. What is it, they asked, that we want? And the answer was: We want a law, which shall keep us near Yahwe, and separate us from the other nations. So they began to gather up all the old laws, and make new ones, and write them down. And of course, along with this, the priests became very important persons. At last, indeed, they became the most powerful class in the nation; the more that the political independence of the people was lost. The nation came to be priest-ridden. Yet it is probable that the priests and others who made these laws wished to train the people to be holy, so that they might have the blessing of the holy Yahwe.

2. What Ezra did. — Ezra lived at the time when the collection of religious laws was very nearly completed. As we have seen, it was the Jews in Babylonia who were particularly zealous in this legal study; those who had returned to Palestine were so busy with the bodily labors of a new settlement that they had little time for study of any sort, but the Babylonian Jews had leisure to think and write. Among them Ezra had learned the law. No doubt he was surprised and shocked when he heard from occasional visitors that his brethren in Palestine were not living according to its prescriptions. So he determined to go and teach them, and accordingly got permission from the Persian king (Artaxerxes Longimanus), came to Jerusalem, and began his work. With the aid of Nehemiah he seems to have succeeded in inducing the people to obey certain rules of the law, such as not marrying foreign wives, and keeping the sabbath and the great festivals. He was a reformer, something like Luther. He began a new phase of Jewish life. Exactly how long he worked, and how much he accomplished in his lifetime, we don't know; but from his time it was that the Jews became "the people of the book." We must describe this book.

3. Formation of the Pentateuch. — In those days (before Ezra's time) the Israelites had no Bible, no collection of sacred books, which they regarded as having been given them by God. Hereafter (Lesson XXIII.) we shall see how their Scriptures (our Old Testament) were gradually gathered together. It was in Ezra's time that this collecting began. We do not know that he himself gathered the laws into a book, — it is more probable that this process had been going on for some time in Babylonia, and that he was only one out of many workers, perhaps a very able and important one. He may have edited, as we now say, almost all of the Pentateuch. Let us look awhile at this book. The word "Pentateuch" (a Greek word, invented long afterwards in Alexandria) means "the fivefold book," that is, the great work which contains the five books, Genesis, Exodus, Leviticus, Numbers, and Deuteronomy. The Jews regarded it as *the* book, the Tora (instruction or law), the foundation and essence of their religion. But these five books were not written all at once; their composition extended over several centuries. From time to time the traditions of the early times (Abraham, Isaac, and Jacob) were committed to writing; this began as early as B.C. 800, or perhaps earlier. Then the accounts of the creation and the first fortunes of the human race were probably learned from the Babylonians during the Exile, and all these stories were put together to form the book of Genesis. Similar traditions concerning the march from Egypt through the wilderness to Canaan constitute the historical part of Exodus and Numbers. At the same time collections of law were being made. About B.C. 750 or 800 some man wrote down a little law book, including in it the chief civil and religious laws of that time. More than a century later (B.C. 622) the legal part of Deuteronomy was composed. After this other usages came into existence, and were set down in books. As the ideas of the temple-worship expanded, the priests would make new prescriptions. So, finally, the books of Leviticus and Numbers and the account of the tabernacle in Exodus were written. Then some one, perhaps Ezra, brought all this material together, and the Pentateuch was formed. And, inasmuch as Moses was looked on as the great lawgiver, all of it was ascribed to him; that is, it was declared to be all the word of God; and, indeed, it was believed by the priests to be necessary to the holiness and happiness of Yahwe's people, Israel. Many of these ceremonial laws are curious, and deserve study. They were, no doubt, beneficial in their time; but they are of no religious use now; they were superseded by the principles that Jesus taught.

4. Character of the Pentateuch. — The Pentateuch may almost be said to be an epitome of the religious history of ancient Israel. Some of its narratives (not traditions, but probably reliable history) go back to B.C. 1000 or 1200, or even earlier. Some of its customs and laws are equally old. On the other hand, it contains laws and perhaps narrations which came into existence after the Exile, as late as the middle of the fifth century B.C. Its growth is parallel to that of the nation. It is the Israelitish Thesaurus, or Treasury of Traditions and Laws. Each narrative or collection of laws bears the impress of the age in which it originated; the whole is a panorama of the religion of Israel. Careful examination of the Pentateuch shows that its different parts are distinguished by the use of different divine names, some having *Elohim* ("God" in the English version), others *Yahwe* (THE LORD in the English version); see Gen. i., ii., iii., and iv. The Yahwe-parts are the older; the Elohim-portions were written after the people began to drop the local, national name of the deity, and adopt the general designation "God." The history of the Flood, for example (Gen. vi.–ix.), is made up from two distinct narratives. On looking at it you will see that sometimes "God" and sometimes "The Lord" is used, and there are other differences corresponding to these. Thus in chapter vi., verses 11–13 describe the same thing as verses 5–7 (in verse 5 instead of GOD read THE LORD); vii. 1–5 goes over the same ground as vi. 14–22.

From this time on the religious history of the Jews is inseparably connected with the Pentateuch. From it they draw their inspiration of mind and soul; it furnishes their philosophy as well as their religion.

LITERATURE.

1. On Ezra and his works: the commentaries and dictionaries. His legendary history is given in Fourth Esdras (Second Ezra).

2. On the origin and construction of the Pentateuch: the Introductions of DeWette-Schrader and Bleek-Wellhausen; articles "Bible" and "Pentateuch" and articles on the several books of the Pentateuch in the Encyclopædia Britannica.

QUESTIONS.

To what point must we now go back? What shall we have to ask?

1. How did the Israelites get on before they had a written law? What happened as society became better organized? As devotion to Yahwe increased, what was more strongly felt? How was this feeling strengthened? What did the more thoughtful men think they wanted? What did they begin to do? Who then became important? What is meant by being priest-ridden? Did the priests have a good motive in what they did?

2. At what time did Ezra live? What Jews were particularly zealous in the study of the law? Why not those of Palestine? What was Ezra surprised to hear? What did he do? Did he succeed in his attempt? Was he a reformer? Like whom? Do we know exactly what he accomplished in his life-time? What was true of the Jews from his time?

3. Had the Jews a Bible before Ezra's time? What do you mean by a Bible? When did the collecting of the Scriptures begin? Was it he who collected them? What may he have done? What is the meaning of the word Pentateuch? What books does it comprise? How did the Jews regard it? Were these books all written at once? Can you tell how the book of Genesis arose? — the historical part of Exodus and Numbers? When was the first collection of laws made, so far as we know? What followed next? What then? What books came thus to be written? How was the Pentateuch then formed? To whom was it ascribed? Why? What did this signify? What did the priests believe? What may be said of the ceremonial laws?

4. What may the Pentateuch be said to be? How early are some of its narratives and laws? How late are others? What would you say of its growth? What is meant by calling it a thesaurus? In what sense is it a panorama? How are its different parts distinguished? What are the two divine names? Which parts are the older? What example can you give of a narrative made out of two other narratives? From this time what is true of the religious history of the Jews?

LESSON XIX.

LITERATURE OF THE EZRA PERIOD.

The Period of Ezra. — For several hundred years after the Restoration (the return to Canaan) the Jews of Babylonia and Palestine were chiefly occupied with working out their Law; their religious mission was to fix the rules of religious life which they believed had been divinely revealed to them. Ezra and his friends, as we have seen, composed the Pentateuch; and his disciples after him for two hundred years continued to study it zealously. We may therefore call this period (say B.C. 500-250) by his name. Besides the prophets already mentioned (Lesson XVII.) this period produced several interesting books of which we must now say a word.

1. The Book of Chronicles. — The book of Chronicles is a history of Judah, composed or finished about B.C. 300. As early as the middle of the Exile there had been written a history of the whole nation, from the time of the Judges down to the carrying away to Babylon; this history is given in the books of Judges, Samuel, and Kings (see Lesson XV.). But it was composed before the final Pentateuchal legislation; it breathes the spirit of the prophets and the book of Deuteronomy, that is, it lays little stress on the ceremonial law. But a change had now come over the nation. The temple-ritual had been introduced. All the details of the service, such as the offerings and the singing, were now thought to be very important. Naturally those who had become used to these things supposed that they had always existed. It was equally natural to wish to have a history of the temple from the beginning. So, after a while, some pious priest or Levite sat down to compose a history of the kingdom of Jerusalem, in which the temple was situated. This history (our book of Chronicles) goes over the same ground as Second Samuel and Kings. But it leaves out much that they have, and puts in much that they have not. It leaves out a good deal of the political and personal history; it puts in a great deal relating to the temple-service. The author cites older writings; but he fills up the picture according to his own ideas. Thus the book is not valuable as a history of the kingdom of Judah; we cannot usually rely on it where it differs from Samuel and Kings. But it is very valuable as an exposition of the ideas of the author's own time. It shows us that some of the Jews then attached more importance to temple-ceremonies than to any other part of religion.

2. The Books of Ezra and Nehemiah. — The books of Ezra and Nehemiah formed originally one book, and were, moreover, a part or a continuation of Chronicles. It brings the history down to the Exile and mentions the Restoration; they begin with the Restoration, and come down to the end of Nehemiah's government (about B.C. 430); they also give a list of priests down to the time of Alexander the Great (Neh. xii. 10, 11). Their object is to describe the building of the second temple, and the enforcement of the Law by Ezra and Nehemiah. This was, in fact, the introduction of the complete ceremonial law. It was the founding of the new Jewish Church.

3. **The Book of Jonah.** — In contrast with this legal literature is another work, which may be assigned to this period, though its exact date is uncertain. The story of the book of Jonah is familiar to us all. The prophet is sent to preach the wrath of God to the great city of Nineveh. The people repent and God pardons them. At this the prophet murmurs; but God teaches him that it is right to be merciful even to the heathen. Thus, while the legalists were building a wall of ceremonies between Israel and the other nations, the unknown author of this little book taught that God's mercy is not bounded by national lines. It is a teaching worthy of the New Testament (see Matt. xii. 41). The hero of the story is the prophet of the time of Jeroboam II. (2 Kings xiv. 25), but the book is a religious apologue composed long after this. Its religious value is independent of the adventures in chapter i.

4. **The Book of Esther.** — The book of Esther was written to give an account of the Jewish feast of Purim, which is still celebrated on the 14th and 15th days of the month Adar (about the first of March). It is referred to in 2 Maccabees xv. 36, under the name of the day of Mardochæus (Mordecai). This feast commemorates a deliverance of the Jews from a Persian persecutor, and is highly valued by them. But the book breathes no pure religious spirit; it contains nothing but hatred and revenge. The name of God does not occur in it, and it says nothing of prayer. It is merely a record of national feeling. To make up for its religious deficiencies, some chapters containing prayers were afterwards added to it; these are found in the Greek version, but not in the Hebrew. The story is laid in the time of the Persian king Xerxes (Ahasuerus). It is hardly reliable history.

5. **The Book of Job.** — It is probably to this period (though it may be a hundred years earlier) that we are to assign a re-

markable book (Job), which introduces us to a new species of literature and a new phase of Israelitish thought. Israel had not only prophets, who preached trust in and obedience to Israel's holy God, and priests, who directed his worship in the temples, but also wise men or sages, who studied philosophy. By philosophy we mean the explanation of man's soul, of human life, and of the world. The Israelitish philosophers seem to have confined themselves at first to giving short descriptions of facts of life, and rules for its guidance, in the form of apothegms or proverbs (see Lessons XXI. and XXII.). Afterwards they discussed wider questions, and especially whether goodness is always rewarded with outward prosperity in this world. The great mystery was that sometimes good men seem to suffer, and bad men to be prosperous and happy; how could a holy God permit this? For a long time the sages explained this by saying that good men were always eventually rewarded and bad men always came to a bad end (see, for example, Ps. lxxiii.). Nobody said anything of a future life; on this point the ancient Israelites had very dim ideas. But this explanation was not satisfactory to all thinkers; it is, in fact, not true. It did not satisfy the author of the book of Job, and he looks for some other solution. The plan of the book is this. A rich and powerful sheikh or pastoral prince is suddenly overwhelmed with misfortunes; he loses his property and his children, and is afflicted with loathsome leprosy. Three of his friends come to condole with him (chapters i., ii.). Then they fall to discussing his case, — why was he thus stricken? The three friends give the old explanation: it was, they said, because he had been a great sinner, and this suffering was the just punishment of his sins. He answered that he was not a great sinner; that he had, on the contrary, been upright, and that he would prove it, if he could only see God, and plead his cause face to face. Finally, however, he affirmed his confidence in God (iii.-xxxi.). Then, in the original form of the poem, followed the address of Yahwe (xxxviii.-xli.), in which he sets forth his power, and leaves Job to infer that he is to submit to God's providences without being able to understand them. And at the end, Job regains prosperity and happiness (xlii.). Afterwards an addition was made to the argument; another speaker (Elihu) was introduced, who affirmed that the object of suffering is to make men better (xxxii.–xxxvii.). So the argument of the book is not conclusive; but it contains noble religious sentiments (especially emphasizing trust in God), and it shows us how earnestly one part of Israel were at this time seeking to know the ways of God with men. God spoke to his people and to us no less through the sages than through the prophets and the priests. The book of Job is one of the most splendid poetical productions of the world. The narrative portion (chapters i., ii., xlii.) is only a frame-work for the religious argument. There may have been a man named Job who suffered great misfortunes; but the scenes in which Satan appears, and the speeches of Job and his friends and of Yahwe, are the invention of the author of the book.

LITERATURE.

1. On Chronicles: see Lesson VII. The works on Introduction may be consulted for all books.

2. On Ezra and Nehemiah: Bertheau's Commentary, and articles in encyclopædias and dictionaries.

3. On Jonah: the commentaries on the Minor Prophets, and the books on Prophecy.

4. On Esther: "Kurzgefasstes Exegetisches Handbuch;" articles in cyclopedias.

5. On Job: commentaries of Delitzsch, Merx, Cox, Lange; articles in cyclopedias; W. H. Green's "Book of Job;" Renan's French translation; Froude, "Short Studies," L

QUESTIONS.

How were the Jews of Babylonia and Palestine occupied after the Restoration? What was their mission? What did Ezra and his friends and disciples do? Why may we call this the Ezra period? What is its date? What books were then written?

1. What is the book of Chronicles? About when was it written? What history of the whole nation was before this in existence? What spirit did it breathe? What change had now come over the people? What did those who had been used to these things think? What did they wish? What

did a priest or Levite do? Over what ground does this history go? What does it leave out? What does it put in? What does the author do? Is the book valuable as a history of the kingdom of Judah? How is it valuable? What does it show?

2. What is the relation of the books of Ezra and Nehemiah to Chronicles? Where does Chronicles end? Where do Ezra and Nehemiah begin? [Compare 2 Chron. xxxvi. 22, 23, with Ezra i 1-3.] What list of priests do they give? What is their object? What was this in fact?

3. What book stands in contrast with this legal literature? What is the story of the book? What did its author teach? Is this worthy of the New Testament? Who is the hero of the story? Was the book composed by him? Of what is its religious value independent? Can you explain what you mean by this?

4. For what purpose was the book of Esther written? Where is this feast mentioned? What was it intended to commemorate? What is its spirit? What does not occur in it? How did this happen? [The author was thinking wholly of the event he was describing, as a national triumph.] What were afterwards added to it? Where are these found? In what time is the story laid? Is it reliable history?

5. What other book is probably to be assigned to this period? Does it belong to a different sort of literature from that we have been considering? What writers did Israel have besides priests and prophets? What did the prophets do?—the priests? What did the sages study? What is philosophy? To what did the Israelitish philosophers at first confine themselves? What question particularly did they afterwards discuss? What was the great mystery to them? How did they explain it for a long time? In what Psalm is the explanation given? [Read the Psalm.] Did they speak of a future life? Why not? [We shall see how they gradually got clearer ideas.] Was this explanation satisfactory to all persons? Did it satisfy the author of the book of Job? Do we know who he was? [No.] What is the plan of the book? Can you point out the divisions by chapters? Does the book after all explain why good men sometimes suffer, and bad men are sometimes prosperous? Can you explain this? What does the book contain? What does it show us? How did God speak to his people? What is to be said of the book of Job as poetry? What of the narrative portion? Was there a man named Job? What parts of the book are the composition of the author?

LESSON XX.

THE HASMONEANS.

The Struggle for Freedom. — In a former Lesson (XVII.) we have followed the political history down to the point where Judea fell under the control of the Greek kingdom of Syria. We must now describe the Jews' struggle for freedom, and the fortunes of the native dynasty that thence arose; it is a time of splendid heroism, when for one brief moment the national life flamed out gloriously before it sank forever under the iron power of Rome.

1. **Antiochus Epiphanes.** — While the successors of Alexander had been quarrelling among themselves over his empire, the Roman republic had been slowly gathering strength, and now, having conquered its neighbors in Europe, had begun to interfere in the affairs of western Asia. It acted as arbiter and judge between rival powers. However, it did not always interfere in the internal management of the various kingdoms. It allowed Syria to govern Judea; and after a while the Jews rebelled against Syrian oppression. It happened in this way. In the year 175 B.C. Antiochus IV., called Epiphanes (the illustrious), ascended the throne of Syria. He was a man not without military skill and administrative capacity, but extravagant, inordinately ambitious, cruel, and bent on carrying out his plans without regard to the rights or comfort of others. Vexed at the failure of one of his attacks on Egypt (when the Romans interfered and stopped him), he vented his anger on the Jews, many of whom he put to death. Finally he determined to force them to give up their own religion, and adopt his. He carried off the sacred vessels of the temple, and built an altar to Zeus (Jupiter) on the altar of burnt offering in the temple-court; he caused swine's flesh to be sacrificed in the sacred place; he forbade the people to circumcise their children; and he tried to destroy the sacred books. The Jews bore loss of property and of life; but they could not give up the religion of their fathers. They revolted.

2. The Two Jewish Parties. — But not all the people opposed the designs of the Syrian king. They were divided into two parties, one of which was favorable to foreign ideas, while the other was bitterly hostile to them. The former was the Hellenizing party; those who belonged to it adopted Grecian names, introduced games and gymnasiums, and tried to be as much like Greeks as possible. The other was the national party, who believed in holding to the customs of their forefathers; they were also called the Hasidim, that is, the Pious. We see it was a dispute very much like that between the prophets and the Baal-worshippers long before (Lesson IX.). The Hellenizing party aided Antiochus in his designs, and the Samaritans sent word to him that they were unconnected with and hostile to the Jews.

3. The War of Freedom. — The national party were determined to resist the king. War was brought on, very much as in the American Revolution (battle of Lexington). One day a Syrian (Greek) officer came to a little place called Modin to set up the Grecian worship there. An old priest named Mattathias slew him, and then fled with his friends to the wilderness. Here, aided by his five valiant sons, he kept up a war against the Syrians. After his death his son Judas became the leader of the national party. He is the hero of the war. Fertile in invention, able in action, with a courage that nothing could daunt, ardently devoted to the religion of Israel, he was the idol of the patriots, and the saviour of his country. Over and over again he defeated large bodies of Syrians with a handful of troops. He recovered Jerusalem, and purged the temple of idols. Meantime King Antiochus died, and in December, 164 B.C., the temple was dedicated anew to the God of Israel, and a feast instituted in commemoration of the happy event. This was the Feast of the Dedication of which we read in the New Testament (John x. 22). From his bravery Judas received the name of Maccabæus (which perhaps means "the hammer"), and his family are thence called the Maccabees, and this period the Maccabean age. He fell in battle, and was succeeded by his brothers Jonathan and Simon. The latter was a wise and good man; under him the Syrians made a treaty with the Jews, and he sent an embassy to Rome, which was favorably received. The independence of the nation was now established; Simon became the chief political and religious officer (prince and high-priest).

4. The Hasmonean Dynasty. — Thus was established a native Judean dynasty of priest-princes. They were called Hasmoneans (or Asmoneans), the origin of which name is uncertain. Simon died B.C. 135. His son, John Hyrcanus I., conquered the Idumeans (Edom), and destroyed the Samaritan temple on Mount Gerizim. John's son Aristobulus is said by Josephus to be the first of the line who assumed the title of king. Now began the decline of the little kingdom. After Aristobulus came his brother, Alexander Jannæus, whose sons, Hyrcanus and Aristobulus, after his death disputed the crown between them. The Romans interfered, and Pompey captured Jerusalem (B.C. 64), but did not hold it. Finally Julius Cæsar took the kingdom from the Jewish princes, and made the Idumean Antipater procurator or governor; this Antipater had been the minister or chief adviser of King John Hyrcanus II.; we shall hear more of his son Herod. So ended the Hasmonean dynasty.

5. The Three Sects or Parties. — During this period arose the sects or parties of the Sadducees, the Pharisees, and the Essenes, the two first of which are often spoken of in the Gospels. The significations of these names are not well understood. The Sadducees were the rich and aristocratic people, who were in favor of maintaining the national life, but at the same time adopting the culture of the Greeks; many of the priests belonged to this party. The Pharisees were the strict, exclusive national party. They hated foreigners and foreign ideas. They made much of the ceremonial part of religion, and of the traditional explanations of the Law that had been slowly growing up. The Essenes were given to ascetic observances. They lived in separate communities, held all property in common, did not marry, and spent all their time in religious acts, such as bathing, reading the Scriptures, praying, and meditating.

LITERATURE.

1. On the history: The first and second books of Maccabees, of which the first is the more reliable; Josephus's Antiquities; the histories of Ewald, Milman, Stanley, Graetz, and E. H. Palmer, London, 1874; Condor's "Judas Maccabæus;" Jost, "Geschichte des Judenthums," books i and ii., Leipzig, 1857; Schneckenburger's "Neutestamentliche Zeitgeschichte," Frankfort, 1862; and similar works by Hausrath, Heidelberg, 1868, and Schürer, Leipzig, 1874.

2. On the parties: the same works; Wellhausen, "Pharisäer und Sadducäer," Greifswald, 1874; A. Geiger, "Das Judenthum und seine Geschichte," Breslau, 1865; articles in cyclopedias.

QUESTIONS.

How far have we followed the political history? What is now to be described? What was the character of the time?

1. What people had been slowly gathering strength? What had it begun to do? As what did it act? Did it allow Syria to govern Judea? What did the Jews do? Who ascended the throne of Syria, B.C. 175? What was his character? When did he vent his anger on the Jews? What did he finally determine to do? How did he proceed? How did the Jews take this?

2. Did all the people oppose the designs of Antiochus? Into what two parties were they divided? What are the names of these parties? How did the Hellenizers act? [To Hellenize means to act like a Greek.] What did the national party believe in? What earlier dispute was this like? Did the Hellenizers aid the king? What did they tell him?

3. What was the national party determined to do? How was war brought on? What happened when the officer came to Modin to set up the worship of Greek gods? After the death of Mattathias, who became the leader of the national party? What was his character? Was he often successful in battle? Did he recover Jerusalem? [The Syrians had taken possession of the city.] What feast was instituted? When? To commemorate what? Where is it mentioned in the New Testament? What name did Judas receive? Why? What are his family called? What is this period called? Who succeeded Judas? What was the character of Simon? What did he accomplish? Was the nation now independent? What did Simon become?

4. What was thus established? What were they called? When did Simon die? What did his son Hyrcanus do? What title did Aristobulus

assume? In the quarrels that afterwards arose among the Jewish princes, what power interfered? What Roman general took Jerusalem? Whom did Julius Cæsar make procurator? What had Antipater been? Did this end the Hasmonean dynasty?

5. What three sects or parties arose during this period? Which of them are mentioned in the Gospels? Who were the Sadducees? — the Pharisees? What did they hate? What did they make much of? To what were the Essenes given? How did they live? How did they spend their time?

LESSON XXI.

LATER LITERATURE. 1. RITUAL AND DIDACTIC.

The Classes of the Literature. — We have described the literature down to the end of the fourth century B C., the year 300 (Lesson XIX.). We must now speak of certain books that were written or finished after this. Please observe in the case of each book whether it was wholly composed or only brought to completion at this time. This was a period of literary as well as political activity (the two frequently go together), and produced some admirable works. We may divide the literature into three classes: the ritual and didactic; the apocalyptic; and the prophetic and historical. Let us begin with the first of these, in which we shall include Psalms, Proverbs, Ecclesiasticus or the Wisdom of the Son of Sirach, the Wisdom of Solomon, Ecclesiastes, and the Song of Songs.

1. Psalms. — The book of Psalms is the hymn-book of the Jewish Church; it is the collection of sacred songs that were sung in the temple after the return from Babylon. These songs express Israel's deepest religious feeling; they are the cries of souls filled with longing after God; they are the voice of God speaking in the hearts of his servants. They set forth the personal experience of the soul in its striving after communion and oneness with the Father of our spirits; they sing of sorrow for sin, hope, trust, love. They belong to us and all the world; though the times have changed, these old hymns continue to furnish us with a high and true expression of our religious emotions. As to their poetical character, they are rhythmical, sonorous, sweet, in the English translation as well as in the Hebrew. They were sung by choirs composed of Levites and women. They had no musical parts except octaves; the melodies, which were very simple, have probably survived in part in our Gregorian chants. It is probable that some of the Psalms were written as early as King Hezekiah's time (about B.C. 700); and they continued to be composed during the Exile (see Lesson XVI. paragraph 4), and afterwards down to and during the Maccabean war of freedom (Ps. xliv., lxxiv., lxxix. seem to belong to the Maccabean period). The inscriptions or titles, which give the authors and occasions. do not belong to the Psalms themselves; they were prefixed later by editors, and are not reliable. Many of the Psalms are ascribed to David, but it is not probable that he wrote any of them. We find out their dates by observing what periods of the history their contents best agree with. From time to time collections of existing psalms were made. Five of these books are indicated in our Psalter: 1. Ps. i.–xli.; 2. Ps. xlii.–lxxii.; 3. Ps. lxxiii.–lxxxix.; 4. Ps. xc.–cvi.; 5. Ps. cvii.–cl. You will find short doxologies at the end of each of these books, except the last, of which the concluding Psalm is itself a doxology. Finally, all the books were gathered into one, perhaps about the year 150 B.C., and that is our book of Psalms. The Greek version (Septuagint) has an additional Psalm, said to be a description by David of his combat with Goliath (1 Sam. xvii.), and also, in some copies, another later psalm-book called the Psalter of Solomon, inferior in tone to our Psalms (about B.C. 45).

2. Proverbs. — In a former Lesson (XIX.) we saw the nature of the Israelitish philosophy, how it dealt with questions of moral and religious life. The sages were accustomed to give their instruction in the form of aphorisms or proverbs; people then had no books, and could more easily remember these short sayings. You will find such sayings in the book of Proverbs, chapters x.–xxx.; chapters i.–ix. and xxxi. are more connected discourses. There is much deep wisdom in these proverbs; some good men have found it well to take one of them every day as a motto for the day, to think about and follow. We do not know exactly when they were composed or collected. It is said that some of them were gathered in Hezekiah's time (Prov. xxv. 1). Most of them were ascribed by tradition to Solomon, as so many of the Psalms were ascribed to David. Solomon may have gathered wise men about him, and encouraged them to put their views of life into the form of proverbs, and may himself have been a sage. Parts of our book of Proverbs were probably composed in the Greek period, and the whole was probably collected about the same time as the Psalms.

3. Ecclesiasticus ; or, the Wisdom of the Son of Sirach. — At this time the Jews were much inclined to compose such books. About B.C. 190 a man named Jesus gathered together some sayings of wise men that he had heard, and added some of his own ; and about sixty years later (probably B.C. 132) his grandson, Jesus, the son of Sirach, edited his grandfather's work, probably adding something to it. This is the book that is called Ecclesiasticus, or sometimes simply the Son of Sirach. It is very much like Proverbs, but also differs somewhat from it. It is distinctively Jewish : it delights in the service of the temple, and puts Israel's happiness in obedience to the Lord; and it confines itself to the present life. It has allusions to the customs of the late time in which it was written. It contains a good deal that is valuable. The common abbreviation of the name Ecclesiasticus is "Ecclus." This book is not in the Hebrew Canon.

4. The Wisdom of Solomon. — Of the same general nature is another book which was written about this time, — the Wisdom of Solomon. It is a long hymn in praise of godly wisdom, and has many excellent precepts for the guidance of life. But it differs from the Son of Sirach's work in two important respects. It is less distinctively Jewish ; indeed, it has a tinge of Greek thought (it was probably written in Alexandria), — a broad, philosophic tone. It speaks of Wisdom almost as if it were a person (very much as Prov. viii. 12–36). And, secondly, what is more important, it distinctly teaches that man is immortal. It is the earliest Jewish book, so far as we know, that does this. In the Pentateuch, the Prophets, the Psalms, and the other books of the Old Testament, except Daniel, future existence is spoken of as almost non-existence. Sheol, the underworld, to which all men are supposed to go after death, is described as a cheerless place, where there is no activity and no hope. But this book says that "God created man to be immortal, and made him to be an image of his own nature" (ii. 23). It was only gradually that Israel came to a clear knowledge of immortality. The Wisdom of Solomon is not in the Hebrew Canon.

5. Ecclesiastes ; or, the Preacher.—The most remarkable of this class of works is that which is commonly called Ecclesiastes (abbreviated for reference into "Eccles."). It is a discussion of human life, put into the mouth of King Solomon, according to the custom of the time, which liked to rest its wisdom on the authority of ancient sages. It says nothing of a future life of work and hope, and what it says of this life is marked by a complete absence of enthusiasm. The author expects nothing satisfactory from any human effort. Not only money and power, but even wisdom fails, he says, to make its possessor happy. Everything passes away, and man himself passes away, and leaves no trace behind. So, our author declares, the best thing to do is to enjoy such good things as the bounty of God gives us, and not to vex ourselves with ceaseless efforts after wealth and wisdom. But we are to enjoy ourselves, he says, not foolishly or wickedly ; we are to have the fear of God before our eyes and to do nothing in excess. This is, in many respects, a most excellent philosophy. On one side it approaches the word of Jesus, that we are not to harass ourselves about to-morrow (Matt. vi. 34). It differs from the teaching of Jesus in not having a warm, loving trust in God. The book was probably written in the second century B.C.

6. The Song of Songs.—This is a lyric poem, apparently composed to praise and recommend faithful wedded love. It seems to belong to this period. It has been usually, but improperly, treated as an allegory.

LITERATURE.

1. On the Psalms : the commentaries of Delitzsch (English translation), Perowne, Lange, Olshausen ; Murray's "Origin of the Psalms," New York, 1880 ; Noyes's translation ; Ewald's "Poets of the Old Covenant," English translation.

2. On Proverbs : commentaries of Delitzsch, Lange, Miller, Noyes.

3. On Ecclesiasticus and the Wisdom of Solomon: Lange and the "Kurzgefasstes Exegetisches Handbuch," on the Apocrypha.

4. On Ecclesiastes : commentaries of Lange and the Handbuch ; Renan's translation, Paris, 1882 ; Noyes.

5. On the Song of Songs : German translation and commentary of Graetz ; Noyes.

QUESTIONS.

How far down has the literature been described? In the present period what must be observed in the case of each book? What was the character of this period? Into what three classes may the literature be divided? What books are included in the first ?

1. What is the book of Psalms? What do its songs express? What experience do they set forth? Of what do they sing? To whom do they belong? What is their poetical character? How were they sung? Had they musical parts? What was the nature of the melodies? In what have they survived? How early were some of these Psalms composed? How long did they continue to be composed? Are the inscriptions reliable? To what man are many of the Psalms ascribed? Is it probable that he wrote any? How do we find out their dates? How many partial collections of Psalms do we know of ? Can you point them out in the Bible? What do you find at the end of each book? Will you read these doxologies? Do they belong to the Psalms themselves? [No; they were appended by the editors.] About what time were all the Psalms gathered into one book? What do we find in the Greek version that is not in the Hebrew and English?

1. With what did the Israelitish philosophy deal? How did the sages give their instruction? Why? In what chapters of Proverbs do we find such sayings? Which chapters contain more connected discourses? Can you show this by referring to the book? What may be said of the moral and religious value of these Proverbs? Do we know exactly when they were composed and collected? In whose time were some of them said to be gathered? Can you read the passage that states this? To whom are most

of them ascribed? What may Solomon have done? Were parts of this book probably composed late? About what time was the whole probably collected?

3. Were the Jews disposed to write such books at this time? What did a certain Jesus do? About when did his grandson edit his work? What is this work called? What book is it like? Does it also differ from Proverbs? Wherein is it distinctively Jewish? To what does it confine itself? Does Proverbs also do this? To what customs does it allude? Has it much valuable ethical instruction? What is the common abbreviation of the name?

4. What other book of the same nature was written about this time? What is it? In how many respects does it differ from the Son of Sirach's book? What is the first of these? Where was the book written? How does it speak of Wisdom? What is its second difference from the Son of Sirach? Is immortality clearly taught in the Old Testament except in the book of Daniel? How is Sheol or Hades described? What does this book say? Can you turn to the passage and read it? How did Israel come to a knowledge of immortality? Are these two books, Ecclesiasticus and the Wisdom of Solomon, contained in the Hebrew and English Old Testament? [No.]

5. What is the most remarkable of this class of works? Of what is it a discussion? Put into whose mouth? According to what custom? Does it speak of a future life? How does it speak of this life? What does the author expect from human effort? What does he say of money, power, wisdom, and all things? What does he think the best thing to do? How does he say we are to enjoy ourselves? Is this a good philosophy? Like what word of Jesus Christ is it? How does it differ from the teaching of Jesus? What is the probable date of the book?

6. For what purpose was the Song of Songs apparently composed? Was it written by Solomon? [No.] To what period does it seem to belong? How has it usually been treated? What is an allegory?

LESSON XXII.

LATER LITERATURE. 2. APOCALYPTIC. 3. PHILOSOPHICAL AND HISTORICAL.

Character of the Apocalyptic Literature. — We come now to an entirely new species of literature, — the works which purported to give an apocalypse or revelation of the ultimate future. The prophets had spoken of the future, but only in general terms. The groundwork of their predictions was ethical and religious; they simply declared that Israel should dwell in peace, obedient to the law of the holy Yahwe; their promises of coming prosperity were broad, trustful inferences from the faithfulness of their God. But now the prophetic inspiration had vanished (Ps. lxxiv. 9). Grievous times had come upon Israel. The mighty nations of the world seemed to be pressing them to destruction. What had become, they asked, of the ancient promises of blessing? Had the Lord forgotten his people? Under these circumstances, while some pious people took refuge in prayer and devotion to the law, others sought to encourage themselves and their countrymen by painting brilliant pictures of the future. Usually they went back and gave a sketch of the history of the world, which they represented as grouped around Israel as the centre. The visions were represented as appearing to some ancient seer. They are precise and distinct up to the time of the writer, and then become general and vague. We shall here mention four of these books: Daniel, the Sibyl, Enoch, and Ezra.

1. **Daniel.** — About the year 164 B.C., just before the death of Antiochus Epiphanes (Lesson XX.), an unknown writer, who was well acquainted with Babylonian affairs, undertook to comfort his people in the gloomy condition of things that then existed. He supposed a seer named Daniel, living in Babylon during the Exile, to have a series of visions setting forth the history of the world from the time of the Babylonian empire (Nebuchadnezzar) to the end of things. He sees four kingdoms successively arise; these are the Babylonian, the Median, the Persian, and the Grecian, and under the last the Syrian (especially Antiochus) is particularly spoken of. Of these, the first is destroyed by the second, the second by the third, the third by the fourth, and the fourth by the kingdom of God, that is, Israel. Chapters ii. and vii. give the four kingdoms; chapters viii., ix., and xi. describe Syria especially. The book (written partly in Hebrew, and partly in Aramaic) has an elevated religious tone. It shows, also, an advance in dogma. It contains the first distinct system of angels found in the Old Testament; it represents the various nations as having guardian angels (x. 13,

20, 21). It has also the first mention of the resurrection (xii. 1–3), a doctrine that seems to have been developed among the Jews under foreign influence. Israel added to its stores from all quarters. The Septuagint contains three additions to the Hebrew book: the story of Susanna, the prayer of Azariah and the Hymn of the three princes, and the stories of Bel and the Dragon.

2. The Sibyl.—The ancients gave the name Sibyl to certain prophetesses who were supposed to predict the history of nations. There exists a collection of predictions of this sort (Sibylline Oracles), written by various authors, Jews and Christians, at different times, during a period of several centuries. A part seems to have been composed not long after the book of Daniel. This describes the victory of the worship of the true God over idolatry, the destruction of the wicked at the coming of the Messiah, the conversion of the nations to the service of the God of Israel, and the blessedness of Judah. In it we find the first clear statement of the doctrine of the Messiah. The prophets had spoken of a king or a dynasty under whom Israel would be prosperous; Daniel speaks of a glorious person like a Son of Man (a representation of the saints of the Most High, vii. 13, 22), to whom everlasting dominion was to be given; and the Sibyl represents the deliverer of Israel as a distinct person sent and commissioned by God to give victory to his people. And this idea of a Messiah or Christ (that is, an anointed one) was in existence when the true Messiah came and pointed Israel not to military glory, but to loving obedience to God. It is not improbable that the famous description of the golden age in Vergil's Fourth Eclogue was suggested by the Jewish Sibyl.

3. Enoch.—The greater part of the book of Enoch was written in the second and first centuries before Christ. It represents the old patriarch Enoch (Gen. v. 24) as having had a series of visions in which the coming judgment of the world was disclosed to him. It speaks more distinctly than Daniel of angels, of the Messiah, and of the last times of the world. It was much valued in the early centuries of our era, and is quoted in the New Testament book of Jude, verses 14, 15. Additions were perhaps made to it by Christian writers.

4. Ezra. — To fill out the series we may add a work which treats of the history of Israel, but was written or completed by a Christian in the first century of our era. The visions, supposed to have been seen by the scribe Ezra, predict the overthrow of the nations and the triumph of the righteous. There is a story of Ezra's having been inspired to write out the whole of the sacred books, they having been lost (xiv. 37–48). The book is called Fourth or Second Ezra (or, in the Greek form, Esdras).

5. Other Works. — Various other works produced during this period attest the literary activity of the Jews. We can only mention the most important. 1. Poetical and philosophic. In Alexandria the Jews caught the literary spirit of the Greeks and wrote poetry and philosophy; that is, they tried to treat the material of their sacred books according to Greek methods. A certain Ezekiel composed a tragedy on the deliverance of Israel from Egypt, parts of which are preserved in the works of the Church Father, Eusebius. Aristobulus discussed the Pentateuch philosophically (see Eusebius and Clement of Alexandria). The ethical poem contained in the Sibylline Oracles, which was formerly ascribed to a Greek, Phocylides, is also by a Jew. These attempts were foreign to the Jewish spirit and had little success (see on Philo later). 2. An unknown writer composed a book in imitation of the ancient prophets, and ascribed it to Baruch, the secretary of the prophet Jeremiah. Another, also unknown, wrote a letter, purporting to be addressed by the prophet Jeremiah to the exiles in Babylon, warning them against idolatry. The dates are uncertain. 3. Historical. The First Book of Maccabees is a history of the war of freedom from its outbreak to the death of Simon, the brother of Judas. It was composed not long after the war, and is generally reliable. The Second Book of Maccabees is less trustworthy. It begins the history farther back, in the time of the high-priest Onias, and comes down to the year before the death of Judas Maccabæus (B.C. 161). It was written some time after the First Book, and is designed to defend Jewish religious ideas. See the beautiful story of the seven brothers in chapter iv.

The Third Book of Ezra (or Esdras) begins with King Josiah and the destruction of the temple by the Chaldeans, and then goes over about the same ground as the Old Testament books of Ezra and Nehemiah. Its author probably did not regard these books as canonical. It is called Third Ezra because Nehemiah is sometimes called Second Ezra. 4. Historical romances. The books of Tobit and Judith are tales designed to impress moral and religious lessons. Tobit describes the fortunes of a pious Jewish family among the exiles in Nineveh. Judith tells how a pious and brave woman delivered her people from an invading army. Neither has any value as history.

LITERATURE.

1. On Daniel: commentaries of Hitzig ("Kurzgefasstes Exegetisches Handbuch") and Kranichfeld, Berlin, 1868; "Speaker's Commentary;" Lenormant, "La Divination chez les Chaldéens;" articles in Herzog, Schenkel, Encyclopædia Britannica; Noyes.

2. On the Sibyl: editions of Friedlieb and Alexandre.

3. On Enoch: English translations, Lawrence, Oxford, 1833, and Schodde, "The Book of Enoch," Andover, 1882; German translation, Dillmann, Leipzig, 1853; French translation, Migne, "Dictionnaire des Apocryphes."

4. On Fourth Ezra and the other Apocalyptic books: Hilgenfeld, "Jüdische Apokalyptik."

5. On Ezekiel, and other poets: Delitzsch, "Geschichte der Jüdischen Poesie."

6. On Baruch, Maccabees, Third Ezra, Tobit, Judith: Grimm and Fritzsche on the Apocrypha ("Kurzgefasstes Exegetisches Handbuch") and Lange.

QUESTIONS.

To what species of literature do we now come? How did the prophets speak of the future? What was the groundwork of their predictions? From what were their promises inferences? In these grievous times did the prophetic inspiration still exist? What Psalm speaks of this? What did the people ask? In what did some pious men take refuge? What did others seek to do? How did they represent the history of the world? To whom were the visions represented as appearing? When are they precise, and when are they vague? What four books are here mentioned?

1. In the year 164 B.C., what did an unknown writer undertake to do? What did he suppose? How many kingdoms does Daniel see? What are they? How are these destroyed? Can you point out the visions in the

Bible? What is the tone of the book? Does it show a dogma or teaching that earlier books have not? What does it say of angels? What of the resurrection? Whence did the Jews probably get this doctrine?

2. What does Sibyl mean? What book of this sort have we? By whom written? When was the Jewish part composed? What does it describe? What do we find in it? Of what had the prophets spoken? Of what does Daniel speak? What representation does the Sibyl give? Was the idea of a Messiah in existence among the Jews when Jesus of Nazareth came? To what did he point Israel?

3. When was the book of Enoch written? What does it represent Enoch as having had? Of what does it speak more distinctly than Daniel? When was it much valued? Where is it quoted? Can you read the passage? By whom were additions made to it?

4. When was Fourth Ezra written or completed? By whom? What do the visions predict? What story does the book contain?

5 What spirit did the Jews catch in Alexandria? Have parts of their poetry and philosophy been preserved? Did these attempts of theirs have much success? Why not? What is the book of Baruch? What three historical books do we find? Of what is First Maccabees a history? Is it generally reliable? Is Second Maccabees equally trustworthy? What is its design? What beautiful story does it contain? Have you ever read the story? What ground does Third Ezra cover? Why is it so called? What is the Greek form of the name Ezra? Why is the book sometimes called First Esdras? What is the design of the books of Tobit and Judith? What does Tobit describe? What does Judith tell?

LESSON XXIII.

THE CANON.

1. Definition of Canon. — The word *Canon* is taken from the Greek, and means first a "reed," and then a "rule" by which things are measured. Thus it came to signify those writings which were conformed to the rule or measure of inspiration; it is equivalent to "a collection of sacred books," — books believed to have been given by divine inspiration. When a book is declared by the proper authority among a people to belong to the sacred collection, it is said to be "canonized," and is called a "canonical" book. Not a few of the Asiatic nations had such sacred collections; they were those nations in whom the consciousness of the divine power and government was strong. Among them were the Assyrians, the Hindus, and the Persians; in later times the Arabs had (and still have) their Koran. But no ancient people had so precise a notion of a canon as the Jews, because to no other people was God so deep a reality. The Jewish Canon is the Old Testament; we must now ask how its books were collected. The New Testament is the Christian Canon. The word "testament" is an incorrect translation of a Greek word which properly means "covenant." The "Old Covenant" is God's covenant or agreement with Israel, whereby he promises them his favor; the "New Covenant" is his pledge of favor through Jesus Christ.

2. The Time before Ezra. — We have already seen that a large part of our Old Testament was written before Ezra's time (B.C. 450). All the prophetic writings, the books of Samuel, Judges, and Kings, Deuteronomy, a good many of the Psalms and Proverbs, and perhaps other works, came into existence during this period. But the Israelites then had no idea of a body of sacred writings. These books were no doubt circulated and read to some extent, particularly by the priests and prophets, and were valued as words of Yahwe, or as helpful to religious life. But there was no attempt to make a separation among the various books that were written, and to declare some to be sacred and authoritative. We know that other books, besides those in our Old Testament, were then composed and are now lost. Time sifted these works, and only the more important were preserved. Gradually, as the ideas of religion among the Israelites became distincter, and as their hopes of political success became dimmer, their attention was fixed on the books that related to religion, and they began to study them more. The old prophetic spontaneousness died out soon after the return from exile, and the people lived more and more in the past, and therefore in the books which rested the present on the authority of the past.

3. The Pentateuch. — Naturally, the first thing to which attention was directed was the Law. During the Exile the leaders of the people came to feel that it was this that most separated Israel from the other nations, and constituted its true life. The Babylonian Jews had devoted much time to collecting and completing the regulations concerning public worship and civil life. At that time no distinction was made between civil and religious law, for did not Yahwe, the God of Israel, order the whole conduct of his people, whether in their duty to him or to one another? The lawyers were also the theologians. Along with the law the traditions concerning the Hebrew ancestors and the first ages of the world were collected. By successive editors all this material was at last brought together and shaped into one book, our Pentateuch. When and by whom the present division of this work into five books was made, we do not know. It had already been done when the Greek translation was made, about B.C. 275. Sometimes the book of Joshua was added, and then the whole was called the Hexateuch (that is, the sixfold book). About Ezra's time the most of the Pentateuch had been formed into a book. He was deeply convinced that this book should be made the nation's rule of life. He came from Babylon to Jerusalem to press this fact on the people. His efforts, seconded by those of Nehemiah, were successful. He began the work, and after a while the whole people felt that the book of the Law was that which God had given them to be the guide of their life. So the Pentateuch, which contained the *Tora* or Law, became a canonical book.

4. The Prophetical Books. — For some time the Pentateuch constituted the whole Canon. Then, as the people continued to study their past history, the words of the prophets, who spoke to them of Yahwe's threatenings and promises, seemed to them more and more important. These also, they said, are words of God to Israel. And as the historical books described Yahwe's dealing with his people, and were written by prophetic men, these also were included in the same category. Thus a second canon was formed, the prophetical. The books of Judges, Samuel, and Kings were called the Former Prophets, and the prophetic books proper the Latter Prophets. The works of the prophets were edited or collected, not always carefully.

Anonymous writings were put into the same manuscript with some known prophet, and after a while came to be regarded as his. Thus the prophecy, Is. xl.–lxvi., is included in the same book with the Isaiah of Hezekiah's time, though it was written during the Exile; and Zech. ix.–xi. and xii.–xiv. are appended to Zechariah's writings, though they do not belong to him. The Prophets thus became canonical, but were not thought so authoritative as the Pentateuch.

5. The Hagiographa. — The Law and the Prophets for a long time formed the Canon. Down to New Testament times the expression "the law and the prophets" was even used for the whole Old Testament; see Matt. v. 17, Luke xxiv. 27, Rom. iii. 21. But other religious books were written after the prophetic canon was formed. There were the Psalms, Job, Ezra, and the other books, which you can find for yourselves in the Old Testament. After a while, towards the close of the second century before Christ, these were gathered into a third partial canon. They were called by the Palestinian Jews simply Writings (ketubim), and by the Greek-speaking Jews Sacred Writings (hagiographa). But there was not perfect agreement among the learned Jews as to all of them. The canonical authority of Ezekiel, Ecclesiastes, and the Song of Songs was still in dispute after the death of the Apostle Paul; but they were finally accepted by the Sanhedrin. The third class of writings was not valued so highly as the other two. The Hebrew Bible arranges the books by the three canons or collections: the Pentateuch, the Prophets, the Writings. The Greek and Latin versions changed the order, and our Bible follows them.

6. The Alexandrian Canon. — What we have been saying refers to the Palestinian Jews. The Jews who lived in Egypt admitted into their Canon a number of other books; it is they that are called the Apocrypha; you will find them printed in some copies of the Bible. They are First and Second Ezra, Tobit, Judith, Additions to Esther, Wisdom of Solomon, Ecclesiasticus, Baruch, Epistle of Jeremiah, Additions to Daniel, Prayer of Manasseh, First and Second Maccabees. On these see the preceding Lesson. All of these are instructive and worthy of study. They were never received as canonical by the Palestinian Jews, because they were not believed to be written by authoritative men. Catholics now accept them as canonical, and most Protestants reject them. Each of them must be judged on its own merits.

7. **The Samaritan Canon.** — The Samaritans had adopted the Israelitish worship, but they withdrew from religious fellowship with the Jews soon after the Pentateuch was made canonical, and before the prophetical and other writings had been included in the Canon. They therefore held to the Pentateuch. alone as sacred.

LITERATURE.

On the Canon: articles in Herzog, Schenkel, Encyclopædia Britannica; books of Introduction; Julius Fuerst, " Der Kanon des Alten Testaments," &c., Leipzig, 1868; Samuel Davidson, " The Canon of the Bible," London, 1877.

QUESTIONS.

1. What does the word canon mean? What did it come to signify? To what is it equivalent? When is a book said to be canonized, and called canonical? What ancient nations besides the Jews had canons? What sacred book have the Arabs and other Mohammedans now? Why did the Jews have a preciser notion of a canon than other ancient peoples? What is the Jewish Canon? What is the Christian Canon? Whence comes the word Testament? What is the Old Covenant? — the New Covenant?

2. Were many books of the Old Testament written before the time of Ezra? Which? Had the Israelites at that time the idea of a body of sacred writings? Were these books circulated and read? By whom? What was not attempted? Were other books then composed, besides those that we have? What became of them? In what proportion was the attention of the Jews fixed on their religious books? When did the prophetic spontaneousness die out? In what did the people then live more and more?

3. What was the first thing to which attention was directed? What did the leaders of the people come to feel during the Exile? To what did the Babylonian Jews devote much time? Was a distinction then made between civil and religious law? Why not? Besides the law what traditions were then collected? Into what book was all this material shaped? Do we know when the present division into five parts or books was made? At what

time had it been already done? When the book of Joshua was added, what was the whole called? In whose time had most of the Pentateuch been formed into a book? Of what was he convinced? For what purpose did he come from Babylon? Were his efforts successful? What did the people after a while feel? What did the Pentateuch thus become?

4. What constituted the Canon for some time? As time went on, what books seemed to the Jews more and more important? What other books were included in the same category with the discourses of the prophets? Why? What second canon was thus formed? What were the historical books called? What were the prophetic discourses called? Were the prophetic writings always carefully collected? Can you give two examples? Was the prophetic canon regarded as equal in authority to the legal (the Pentateuch)?

5. Did the Law and the Prophets long constitute the Canon? Can you turn to New Testament passages in which this expression is used for the whole Old Testament? Were other religious books written after the prophetic canon was formed? Can you mention them? When were they gathered into a third canon? What were they called by the Palestinian Jews? — by the Greek-speaking Jews? Was there perfect agreement concerning them among the Jewish doctors? How late were there disputes about certain books? Was this third part of the Canon so highly valued as the others? What is the order of books in the Hebrew Bible? Whence comes the order in our English Bible?

6. Did the Egyptian Jews admit into their Canon books that the Palestinian Jews rejected? What are they called? Can you mention them? Are they all worthy of study? [They all throw light on the religious and other ideas of their time.] Why were they not received as canonical by the Palestinian Jews? What Christians accept them? Who reject them? How must they be judged?

7. When did the Samaritans withdraw from religious fellowship with the Jews? What book alone did they look on as canonical? Why?

LESSON XXIV.

THE SCRIBES.

1. The Study of the Law. — While the sacred books were being collected, the religion of Israel was undergoing a modification, and entering on what has turned out to be its last stage of development; this is what is called the scribal period. The prophets had labored several hundred years to make Yahwe's righteousness a part of the people's living religious faith; and by the end of the Exile the nation had, largely through them, accepted monotheism. After the Exile Israel was divided into two parts, one in Babylon, the other in Palestine; both devoted themselves to the completion of their ritual law, and each became in a sense a church, or both together formed a church, that is, a community organized on a purely religious basis. They had the spiritual fundamentals of religion, namely, a holy God and obligation to live in communion of soul with him. Next, therefore, they set themselves to work out the rules of outward service; they came under the direction of the priests. This is what happened to Christianity also from the third century to the fifteenth. This was a real advance in religion; it was, indeed, a necessity for that stage of the world's religious growth. For all men require rules, more or less according to their spiritual maturity. Israel was growing in ethical-religious fixedness, was acquiring greater spiritual stamina, and embodied its feeling in regulations for the ordering of life. The priests did a part of this work, and the scribes completed it. They took the Law and made it into a code for the determination of man's conduct every day and every hour. They thus did harm, indeed, as well as good; but they furnished the world with what it needed at that time.

2. Formation of the Class of Scribes. — The Law was completed and introduced by Ezra and his friends, and thenceforward became the chief study of Israel. When it came to be put into practice, many points needed explanation. Occasions presented themselves not contemplated by the framers of the code, and it was necessary to adapt the written regulations to these. Hence there arose a class of students of the law.

As printing was then unknown, all books had to be written out with the hand. This process was not only laborious, but required great carefulness in the writer, and knowledge of the subject-matter of the book; an ignorant copyist would be likely to make mistakes which, in an important work, would be inconvenient and injurious. Thus the writers or scribes were commonly men learned in the ritual code, and so the word "scribe" came naturally to signify a learned legalist or lawyer. After a while such men included the prophets and the other writings, as well as the law, in their study. Precise rules were made for those who copied the manuscripts. They had to prepare themselves for the work by washing and prayer; the words of the Pentateuch and the other books were counted, so that not one should be omitted; and other precautions were taken against error. In this way the later manuscripts were made very accurate, though at first they doubtless contained mistakes. None of the manuscripts written before the beginning of our era have survived. After Ezra's time, when the people felt an increasing interest in their sacred books, and, being scattered through the country, could not easily go up frequently to Jerusalem to worship, religious exercises began to be held at various places on the sabbath-day. A part of the Law would be read and some explanation of it given. These assemblages were called synagogues (which means "assemblages"), and the same name was given to the buildings in which they were held. After the prophetic canon was collected, selections from it also were read in these weekly meetings, and afterwards parts of the other books on certain occasions. The later usage required the presence of ten men to constitute a synagogue. The Pharisees, who were devoted to the maintenance of the national life, naturally became advocates of the study of the law and of the oral explanations of it which the expounders used to give in the synagogues and elsewhere. They would thus be associated with the scribes; and in the Gospels the phrase "scribes and Pharisees" is often used to denote the advocates of the oral tradition. The difference between them is this: "scribe" denotes a profession or calling, like our "lawyer" or "theologian;" "Pharisees" means a party, like our terms "orthodox" or "high-church." A scribe might be a Pharisee or a Sadducee; most of them seem to have been Pharisees. But not all Pharisees were scribes; we may say, speaking generally, that a scribe was a learned Pharisee.

RELIGION OF ISRAEL. 121

3. Schools and Teachers. — At various times eminent teachers of the law gathered their pupils around them and formed schools; but we know little of them till shortly before the beginning of our era. According to the later Jewish tradition, Ezra and the distinguished men of his time established the Great Synagogue, which continued about 150 years, and settled the Canon; but there is no ground for this statement. We have records, however, of several teachers, of whom short sayings are reported. These teachers generally taught in pairs. The most important of these pairs was the one composed of Hillel and Shammai, who flourished about 50 B.C. Shammai insisted on a strict construction of the law, while Hillel favored the broadest interpretation of the rules, and his principles finally prevailed. He is the greatest legal scholar and reformer of this period. He framed a set of rules of interpretation, which the Jews have held to ever since. There had grown up a great mass of traditions relating to the Scriptures, and he arranged these in six divisions or orders (see on the Talmud, Lesson XXVI.). His grandson was Gamaliel, the Apostle Paul's teacher (Acts v. 34, xxii. 3). Hillel was born and brought up in Babylonia. A saying is ascribed to him very much like the Golden Rule of Christ: " Do not to another what you would not like to be done to yourself " (see Matt. vii. 12).

4. The Sanhedrin. — The Jews had numerous local courts for the decision of questions of law. After a while they made a Supreme court which they called the Sanhedrin (this is the Greek word *synedrion*, and means a body of men sitting together; a Council). We do not know exactly the date of its origination. It probably grew up gradually; it seems to have been in existence in the second century B.C., but not to have been fully organized till about the year 100 B.C. It consisted of seventy members (scribes and priests) and a president; the latter was the high-priest, as long as there was a high-priest (up to the destruction of Jerusalem). The Sanhedrin at first had supreme civil and ecclesiastical jurisdiction in Israel. Afterwards its powers were abridged by the Romans. It passed sentence of death on Jesus, but its decision had to be ratified by the Roman governor. It had the ordering of the Jewish calendar.

5. Method and Influence of the Scribes. — The Jews, as we have seen, had gone naturally into the study of their Law, which they believed to be the divinely revealed guide of life. But, in their eagerness to obey it strictly, they became slaves of the letter and forgot the spirit. It was this that Jesus charged against them. Their oral commentary or legal tradition became very burdensome (Acts xv. 10,) and sometimes in effect set aside the Law (Mark vii. 9). Their interpretations of Scripture were often forced and misleading. The result of the scribal study was to formalize religion. On the other hand, the scribes or doctors (rabbis) performed the great work of codifying the oral law. What was more important, their labors helped to produce that ethical-religious vigor which gave the Jews their superiority over the Roman world, and enabled them to impress their purer religious ideas on their contemporaries, and thus prepare the way for Christianity.

LITERATURE.

Histories of Josephus, Ewald, Milman, Jost; Reuss, "Geschichte des Alten Testaments;" Etheridge, "Introduction to Hebrew Literature;" Bleek's "Introduction to the New Testament;" works of Hausrath and Schürer on "Neutestamentliche Zeitgeschichte."

QUESTIONS.

1. What period of the religious history have we now reached? Does this represent a modification of the religion of Israel? Is it the last? What had the prophets labored to do? Had they been successful? After the Exile, into what two parts was Israel divided? To what did they devote themselves? What did they become? What is a church? What had they? What did they next set themselves to do? Was this a real advance? Why? In what was Israel growing? What did the scribes do?

2. By whom was the Law completed? What happened when it came to be put into practice? What class of men thence arose? How were books then made? What did this require? What did the word "scribe" come to

signify? Why? What other writings were afterwards included in the study? What rules were made for copying? Were the later manuscripts thus made accurate? Have we any of the earliest? Can you describe the rise of synagogues? What was the nature of the religious service held in them? Are they frequently mentioned in the New Testament? Are they mentioned in the Old Testament? [Yes, in the late Ps. lxxiv. verse 8.] Why were the Pharisees associated with the scribes? What is the difference between them?

3. Do we know much of the earliest teachers of the Law? What was the Great Synagogue, according to the later Jewish tradition? Is this historical? What are reported of several teachers? How did they generally teach? Which is the most important of these pairs? What was the difference between the two men? What can you say of Hillel? Who was his grandson?

4. What was the Sanhedrin? How did it grow up? Can you give probable dates? Of whom did it consist? What was its jurisdiction at first? Afterwards? What of its sentence on Jesus? Of what had it the ordering?

5. What happened to the Jews in their eagerness to obey their Law? What did their legal tradition become? What was the result of the study of the Law by the scribes? On the other hand, what great work did they perform? What was a more important result of their labors?

LESSON XXV.

THE FALL OF JERUSALEM.

1. The Herod Family. — We have now to relate the destruction of the Jewish nationality, whose history we have followed through more than a thousand years. The Hasmonean kingdom, after a vigorous career of a century, had dwindled down to almost nothing (Lesson XX.). Hyrcanus II. and Aristobulus, the sons of King Alexander Jannæus, had engaged in civil war, and the Romans had been called in ; Pompey had taken possession of Jerusalem (B.C. 64), and Crassus had plundered the temple (B.C. 53). Finally Julius Cæsar made the Idumean Antipater governor of Judea, and his son Herod was afterwards established on the throne ; he reigned from B.C. 37 to A.D. 4 ; in the latter part of his reign Jesus of Nazareth was born. He was a vigorous but despotic and cruel ruler. He was a foreigner, belonging to a people who were hereditary enemies of the Jews; he was attached to the Romans by education and interest, and became their tool. He had no love for the people over whom he reigned. He pitilessly extirpated the royal Hasmonean family, one of whom (Mariamne) he had married. He trampled savagely on cherished Jewish ideas. He did his best to Hellenize and Romanize the nation by introducing Greek and Roman customs, such as public baths and theatrical shows; and a considerable party (the Herodians, Matt. xxii. 16) adhered to him. He was fond of splendid buildings, and, among other things, pulled down the temple and rebuilt it in magnificent style, so that it was one of the wonders of the world (John ii. 20, Matt. xxiv. 1). After a long reign he died of a painful disease, universally execrated. The story told of him in Matt. ii. is quite in accordance with his known character. His reign is a step towards the dissolution of the Jewish nation.

A good many of his descendants are mentioned in the New Testament. On his death his territory was divided by the Roman Emperor (Augustus) among his sons: Archelaus (Matt. ii. 22) had Judea, Samaria, and Idumea (Edom); Herod Antipas or Antipater (Matt. xiv. 1-4) received Galilee and Perea; Philip (Luke iii. 1) was made tetrarch of Iturea and Trachonitis, east of the sea of Galilee. After some years (A.D. 41-44) one of his grandsons, Herod Agrippa I. (Acts xii. 1, 20-23) became king over the whole land. He was friendly to the Jewish religion, as was also his son, Herod Agrippa II. (Acts xx. 13), who had a sort of ecclesiastical control over Judea. There were also noteworthy women in the Herod family, — Herodias (Matt. xiv. 3), Salome (xiv. 6), Drusilla (Acts xxiv. 24), and Berenice (xxv. 13).

2. The Roman Procurators. — Herod's son, Archelaus, was so bad a ruler that he was banished by the Romans (A.D. 6), and Judea was placed under Roman governors or procurators. The fifth of these was the Pontius Pilate (A.D. 26-37), under whom Jesus of Nazareth was crucified. After him came two more, and then Herod Agrippa I., mentioned above, was made king. After his death there were seven more Roman governors, of whom two appear in the book of Acts (xxiv. 27).

3. The Uprising and Fall. — The Jews had never submitted willingly to the Roman government. A party among them, indeed, were favorable to foreign ideas, but the mass of the people sided with the Pharisees, who were strict upholders of the national life, and hated the Romans. Some were constantly on the lookout for opportunity to revolt. There were several local uprisings, which were easily crushed by the Romans. Finally the feeling grew too strong to be held in check. There was not the slightest chance of success against the power of Rome ; but the Jews were desperate. The Zealots, that is, the men who were in favor of immediate revolt, grew daily more numerous. The administration of the fourteenth procurator, Gessius Florus, was particularly oppressive. On the other hand, there was no principle of order in the Jewish people itself. The high-priesthood, which was the natural head of the nation, had become contemptible; high-priests were set up and removed at the will of the civil ruler. There was no conservative force ; the Zealots infected the land with their fanaticism, and the people plunged into war. The history of this war has been written by a man who took part in it, Flavius Josephus ; it would be hard to find a more thrilling narrative than his account of the struggle in Galilee, and the siege and capture of Jerusalem. But there could be only one termination to the unequal combat. The Jews fought like heroes or tigers, and fought in vain. Jerusalem was captured by Titus (A.D. 70), the temple was destroyed, the people were slain or banished, the land was left desolate.
The Jews have never recovered from this blow. They have never, since that time, been possessors of Palestine ; the temple has never been rebuilt ; there has never since been a Jewish nation. But though the *nation* was destroyed, the *people* remained. Scattered over the face of the earth, they have formed a new Israel more remarkable in some respects than the old.

4. Change of Language. — Ever since the Exile the outward circumstances of the Palestinian Jews had been determined by their surroundings. Among other things they had changed their language and their writing. They spoke their own Hebrew tongue, and used the old Phœnician letters up to about B C. 150. But the Aramaic or Syriac language and writing were spreading over all this part of Asia, and the Jews adopted them. In this respect the Aramaic was like the French language to-day, which for some time has been the medium of intercourse between the various nations of Europe ; only the former expelled its neighbors and took their place. For a century or two before the birth of Christ the Palestinian Jews wrote most of their books in Aramaic; it was their vernacular in the New Testament times, — it was spoken by Jesus and his disciples ; it was also the vernacular of the Babylonian Jews, and in it the greater part of the Talmud is written (Lesson XXVI.). In the New Testament it is called Hebrew (John xix. 20, Acts xxii. 2) ; the two languages are about as much alike as English and German. In Alexandria and the rest of Egypt the Jews spoke and wrote in Greek; and generally they adopted the language of the people among whom they lived. Yet, though they thus conformed their speech to that of their neighbors, they continued to be Jews in face and thought.

5. **Christianity.** — During this period the greatest religious movement of the world sprang from the bosom of the Jewish nation. Jesus of Nazareth appeared and taught pure, spiritual religion in Galilee and Jerusalem. His first disciples were Jews, but he exercised little influence on his own people. Christianity was preached among the other nations, and accepted by them ; the Jews retained their own form of religion. All through the New Testament times the Jewish doctors of law were pursuing their own work. They believed that the Law was God's final revelation of truth to men, and it seemed to them that Jesus and his followers were trying to destroy the Law ; they therefore held him to be an enemy of God. Unfortunately for them they could not distinguish between letter and spirit; they could not see that Jesus was only selecting and fixing the permanent elements of the Old Testament teaching, in order to give them to all the world. They were tied down

by their national narrowness. Their religion was the religion of their fathers, of their people; they felt all parts of it to be important, and they would not surrender even its simplest ceremony. So Christianity passed on, and left no trace on Judaism. For a century or two a good many Jews embraced the new doctrine, which meant for them that Jesus of Nazareth was the Messiah promised in the Old Testament; but the nation as a whole, the national development, remained unaffected. Christianity is an unimportant incident in the history of this period of the religion of Israel.

LITERATURE.

1. On the political history: the works of Josephus, Ewald, Milman, Palmer.

2. On the history of culture: Etheridge, " Introduction to Hebrew Literature;" Jost, " Geschichte des Judenthums;" Schürer, " Neutestamentliche Zeitgeschichte."

QUESTIONS.

1. What is now to be related? What had become of the Hasmonean kingdom? What did the Romans do? Who was Antipater? Who was his son? What was Herod's character? Did he love the Jews? How did he treat the Hasmoneans? — and Jewish ideas? Of what was he fond? Was he universally execrated? What story is told of him in Matt ii.? Are many of his descendants mentioned in the New Testament? Can you refer to the passages?

2. When was Judea placed under Roman governors? Who was the fifth of these? What others are mentioned in the New Testament?

3. Had the Jews ever submitted willingly to the Romans? Was there a Jewish party favorable to foreign ideas? What of the mass of the people? Was there a growing disposition to revolt? Was there any chance of success against the Romans? Who were the Zealots? Did they grow more numerous? How did the procurator Gessius Florus increase the disaffection? What was the condition of the Jewish nation? What of the high-priesthood? Who has written the history of the war that followed? When was Jerusalem taken? Have the Jews ever recovered from the blow? Though the *nation* was destroyed, have the *people* remained? What of the new Israel?

4. How long did the Jews continue to use their own language and writing? What did they then adopt? Of what Jews did the Aramaic become

the vernacular? Was this language like the Hebrew? What language did the Egyptian Jews speak? — other Jews? Did the Jews still retain their national appearance and thought?

5. What great religious movement occurred during this period? Did it greatly influence the Jews? What did they believe? How did they look on Jesus? What did they fail to see? By what were they tied down? Did some Jews become Christians? What did Christianity principally mean for them? Is Christianity closely connected with the history of the religion of Israel?

LESSON XXVI.

THE TALMUD.

1. The Later Judaism. — After the time of Ezra the Jews, as has been above described, became people of a book, and that book was the Old Testament, or, more especially, the Tora, or Law, or Pentateuch. But this book needed explanations, and after a while the explanations grew into a book, which gradually practically usurped the place of the Old Testament, and became the chief study of the learned men; this second book was the Talmud. It is the representative work of the later Judaism, as the Old Testament is of the earlier. The prophets had called the people to righteousness and the fear of God in ringing tones; the priests had made a ritual law; the sages had discussed human life; the psalmists had poured out before God their repentance, their fears and trust and hopes, their peace and joy; the scribes and rabbis undertook to turn religion into arithmetic. The Talmud is the code of the later Judaism, comprising both the civil and the religious law. It reflects the spirit, as it formed the study, of the nation at the moment when it rejected Christianity. It is the product of its decaying genius. It is the nation's effort, after its creative power had vanished, to reduce the spirituality of its fathers to rule. Let us look at the two parts of the Talmud: the Mishna, or text, and the Gemara, or commentary.

2. The Mishna. — In Hillel's time the oral explanations of the Law had grown into a great mass. He was gifted with a retentive memory and considerable logical power, and he performed the service of arranging them according to subject-matter in six divisions, called orders. After his death the schools continued to study them in these divisions. Many noteworthy men devoted their lives to the explanation of Scripture, following the rules of interpretation that Hillel had drawn up. The schools, both in Palestine and in Babylonia, were well organized, having presidents and other instructors, two regular sessions or semesters yearly, and public disputations. Up to the destruction of Jerusalem, the chief Palestine school was in that city; it was then removed to Jamnia, on the shore of the Mediterranean, not far from Mount Carmel, where it remained about seventy years, surviving the unhappy insurrection of Barcochba. When it was broken up, a new school was established at Tiberias, on the Sea of Galilee. This place is renowned in connection with the labors of Jewish learned men. Here, for many centuries, they gave their lives to the study of their sacred books, and the community of scholars established there remained up to a few years ago. Here, towards the latter part of the second century, flourished the famous Rabbi Jehuda the Holy, commonly called, by eminence, simply Rabbi. The date of his death is disputed; some give it as A.D. 190, others as A.D. 220. It is he who was the compiler of the Mishna. There was, at this time, a growing feeling that the oral explanations of the Law ought to be committed to writing, lest they should vanish from men's memories; for, up to this time, they had been taught only orally, and not a word of them written down. Several attempts were accordingly made to reduce them to writing; but Jehuda's is the one that obtained general currency, and has been handed down to us. He did for the Jewish law nearly what Blackstone did for the English: he digested and arranged it. His six divisions or orders were those of Hillel. They are: 1. *Zeraim* (Seeds), on prayers, sowing, tithes, and first-fruits; 2. *Moed* (Meeting or Festival), on the Sabbath, Passover, Day of Atonement, Feast of Tabernacles, New Year, Purim; 3. *Nashim* (Women), on laws of marriage and divorce; 4. *Nezikin* (Injuries), on injuries, loans, buying and selling, the Sanhedrin, punishments, oaths, idolatry, and heresy, together with the interesting tract called *Pirke Aboth*, or the Sayings of the Fathers, a collection of sketches of the men who transmitted the oral law; 5. *Kadashim* (Consecrations), on various things connected with sacrifices; 6. *Taharoth* (Purifications), on the rules of purification from ceremonial uncleanness. Each of the six orders is made up of several treatises; there are sixty-three of these in all. The Mishna is the Digest of Jewish law, civil and religious. It is written in Aramaized Hebrew.

3. The Gemara. — After the Mishna was compiled, it became the text for lectures in the schools. Being brief and terse, it also, like the Law, needed explanation, and, in the course of a century or two, it had called forth a large mass of oral commentary, which was handed down from teacher to teacher. This likewise was committed to writing, and in double form, in Palestine and in Babylonia; we have thus the Jerusalem Gemara (that is, tradition) and the Babylonian Gemara. Mishna and Gemara together (text and commentary) form the Talmud; we commonly speak of the Talmuds of Jerusalem and Babylon. Of these the latter is the fuller and more important. The Babylonian Jews, descendants of those who had been carried into captivity by Nebuchadnezzar, had formed renowned schools at Sora, Nehardea, and Pumbaditha, which rivalled, and sometimes outshone, the sister-academy at Tiberias. In the fifth century of our era Rabbi Ashe (called Rabbana) did for the commentary what Jehuda had done for the text: he digested and arranged it; the result was the Babylonian Gemara. The date of the Jerusalem Gemara is uncertain; but it is usually thought to be older than the Babylonian. The language of the Gemara is Aramaic, mixed with foreign words.

4. Contents of the Talmud. — The word "talmud" means doctrine, or teaching, and the book so called is the digest of the Jewish thought of the first centuries of our era, on civil polity, religion, science, and philosophy; it is the Jewish Cyclopedia of Sciences. The disputations of the rabbis, of which the Gemara is a record, traverse a wide and varied field, and are characterized by an amazing mixture of acuteness, narrowness, geniality, profoundness, and nonsense (the same thing may be said of the writings of the Church Fathers). The legal discussions and judicial decisions (called Halacha) are often instructive by their sharp common sense and sound judgment; the ethical and devotional disquisitions and stories (Haggada) are commonly archæologically and philosophically interesting. The religious character of the Talmud corresponds to what has just been said. The book is a faithful reflection of the religion of Israel of that day. It contains much true and lofty religious thought. In it may be found parallels to many of the sayings of Jesus in the Sermon on the Mount and elsewhere. On the other hand, it shows bigotry, narrowness, and pettiness. Especially it is lacking in inspiring power. It conceives of religion too much as a system of rules. In reading it one does not feel the breath of the spirit of God. Its teaching may be very much like that of the New Testament (which was written about the same time and by Jews), but it lacks the life of the New Testament.

5. Other Literature. — Besides the Talmud, various other works, containing commentaries on the Law, were composed or begun about this time; that is, in the five first centuries of our era. They, like the Talmud, contain the two elements, halacha and haggada. To the latter of these the name "Midrash" (investigation or commentary) is sometimes given.

LITERATURE.

1. On the Talmud : histories of Ewald, Jost, Graetz, Herzfeld; Fuerst, "Culturgeschichte der Juden;" Etheridge, "Introduction to Hebrew Literature;" works on the history of New Testament times, by Hausrath and Schürer; article "Talmud" in the works of Emanuel Deutsch; articles in cyclopedias.

2. Translations: Latin translation of the Mishna, by Surenhusius, Amsterdam, 1698–1703; English translation of Eighteen Treatises of the Mishna, by De Sola and Raphall, London, 1845; Barclay, "The Talmud" (17 Treatises), 1878; Schwab, "Jerusalem Talmud" (13 Treatises), Paris, 1871–82 ; A. Wünsche, "Jerusalem Talmud" (Haggada), Zürich, 1880.

QUESTIONS.

1. How did the Talmud usurp the place of the Old Testament among the Jews? How did the work of the scribes differ from that of the old prophets, priests, sages, and psalmists? To what did the Jews endeavor to reduce religion in the Talmud? What are its two parts?

2. What service did Hillel perform? After his death what did the schools do? How were these schools organized? Where was the chief Palestine school up to the destruction of Jerusalem? Where after that? What can you say of Tiberias? What is the date of Rabbi Jehuda? Why did he undertake to arrange the oral tradition? What is the name of the book he composed? Can you mention its six divisions? What is the Mishna? What is a digest?

3. What use was made of the Mishna? Why did it need commentary? In what two countries was this commentary committed to writing? What is it called? What is the Talmud? Who compiled the Babylonian Talmud? When? What of the date of the Jerusalem Talmud?

4. What does Talmud mean? What may the Talmud be called? What is the character of the disputations of the rabbis? What is Halacha?— Haggada? Of what is the Talmud a faithful reflection? Has it lofty thought? Does it contain parallels to the sayings of Jesus? In what is it lacking? How does it conceive of religion? What quality of the New Testament is not found in it?

5. What other works were composed or begun about this time? What two elements do they contain? What is Haggada sometimes called?

LESSON XXVII.

THE REMAINING LITERATURE.

Philo and Josephus. — The Talmud may be called the second Pentateuch. As the Old Testament Pentateuch, or Tora (Law), embodies the old Israelitish religious ideas extending over seven or eight centuries (say from Samuel to Nehemiah), so the Talmud is a collection of the later ideas extending over about six centuries (say from the second century B.C. to the fifth century A.D.), and is a continuation of and commentary on the earlier books. These two books may be said to give the whole history of the religion of Israel; for before the time represented by the Pentateuch Israel was only a half-civilized nation, and after the Talmud nothing new was added by Jewish thought. To illustrate this we may take a general view of the literature of the Israelites after Christ. But first we must mention two famous writers who represent not the spirit of Israelitish thought, but that thought modified or transformed by foreign influence: they are Philo and Josephus. Philo of Alexandria (first half of the first century) adopted the Greek (Platonic) philosophy, which he tried to find in the Law. To do this he was obliged to allegorize the Pentateuch. He influenced Christian rather than Jewish thought. Flavius Josephus (latter half of the first century), born of a priestly family, fought against the Romans, but submitted and went over to them just before the capture of Jerusalem. He became to a great degree Romanized. He wrote the history of Israel in two works, the Antiquities and the Wars of the Jews. These are of prime importance, though he is not always trustworthy. Both these authors wrote in Greek. Let us now look at the Jewish literature proper.

1. Bible Translations. — We have seen how the Jews, soon after the Greek conquest, everywhere gave up their own language (Hebrew), and adopted that of the people among whom or near whom they dwelt. In Egypt and elsewhere they learned to speak Greek; in Palestine they spoke Aramaic or Syriac. Thus the people were unable to understand their Scriptures in Hebrew, and desired to have them translated into the tongue they spoke. From this there resulted in Egypt the Septuagint version (Lesson XVII.); and in Palestine and Babylonia translations were made into Aramaic. These were called *targums*, that is, interpretations or translations. They were at first oral: the synagogue reader used to read the Scripture in Hebrew and then render it into Aramaic for the benefit of the people. After a while, for greater convenience, they were written down. The earliest of these written targums is one of the Pentateuch, dating from the second century of our era; it is called the Targum of Onkelos, and is a simple and generally faithful translation of the Hebrew, and therefore helpful to us in our study. It may be added that about the same time was produced a new translation of the Bible into Greek, by a Jew named Aquila. The Christians, who like the Jews used the Septuagint, employed this version to prove from the prophets the messiahship of Jesus of Nazareth; and the Jews, dissatisfied with the Septuagint, made this new translation on which they might rely against the Christians as a faithful rendering of the original. The version of Aquila, of which fragments remain, is extremely, sometimes absurdly, literal. The name Onkelos is supposed to be a pseudonym, and merely the Hebrew form of Aquila. The next targum after Onkelos is that of Jonathan on the prophetical books; it is less literal, more paraphrastic than the former, and introduces a good many later religious ideas. Then came targums on the other books (Hagiographa), and on the Pentateuch. These are not very valuable as translations. Sometimes they are mere paraphrases, full of rabbinical notions. They are, however, valuable as indications of the ideas of the times in which they were written, and are full of matter interesting to the general reader.

2. The Masora. — The Jews, as has been said, became worshippers of the letter of the Scripture. Every word, every letter, of the Old Testament became sacred in their eyes. This would have been well enough if they had not at the same time shut their eyes to the deeper spiritual meaning of the Bible. The study of biblical words was called *masora*, and the learned men who pursued it were the *Masorites*. What they did was this: 1. It was necessary, of course, that the Scriptures should be read correctly in the synagogue; and therefore they fixed on a standard pronunciation (as our dictionaries try to do). In order to indicate the pronunciation they devised signs for the vowel-sounds; hitherto only the consonants of Hebrew words had been written, thus: *mlk*, which in English you can pronounce only *milk*, might in Hebrew be pronounced *melek*, *molek*, *melok*, *maluk*, or *malak*. They pronounced after the manner of their time, which may not have been exactly that of the time of David and Isaiah. 2. They counted the words and letters of the Old Testament, in order to be sure that none were left out in copying manuscripts. 3. They settled the text of the Scripture, that is, decided that such and such words belonged in certain places and not other words. All manuscripts were then written after the standard copy. All existing Hebrew manuscripts give the masoretic text; and therefore, though about 1,400 are known, they only tell us how the Old Testament was read by the Jews in the sixth century of our era.

3. **Grammars and Dictionaries.** — After the Moslem conquest of Syria, Babylonia, and Egypt (from the seventh century on), the Jews in those regions learned to speak Arabic, and soon felt the need of books which should give the Arabic equivalents for Hebrew words. Then they caught the grammatical spirit from the Arabs, who had got it from the Greeks and Syrians. Many Jews wrote Hebrew grammars and dictionaries, and they have continued this sort of work up to the present day. The most famous of the earlier grammarians is Elias Levita, who was a contemporary of Martin Luther, and the teacher of many Christians; at that time the Christian world was just waking up to the study of Hebrew.

4. **Expository and Philosophical Works.** — Ever since the composition of the Talmud the Jews have been writing commentaries on it and on the Old Testament. There is a good deal of sameness in these works, and for the most part they are not very valuable. (This remark is not meant to apply to recent Jewish commentaries, which follow scientific methods of exegesis.) The most noted commentators on the Bible are Rashi (France, eleventh century), Aben Ezra (Spain, twelfth century), David Kimchi (France, thirteenth century), and Abarbanel (Spain, fifteenth century). The most famous expounder of the Talmud is Maimonides (Spain, twelfth century), called by the Jews Rambam, that is, Rabbi Moses Ben Maimon (R M B M). He was at the same time the boldest and most philosophical of mediæval Jewish writers, ranking, indeed, with the foremost thinkers of that period. The Jews expressed their judgment of him in the saying: "From Moses to Moses there has arisen none like Moses," that is, Maimonides had not his equal since the days of the great lawgiver of Israel. In those days the

Jews learned philosophy from the Arabic translations of Aristotle, and in their turn became the teachers of Christian philosophers. The philosophy of the Jews was thus not their own; it was borrowed from their neighbors. So it has been ever since. They have followed the movements of the peoples among whom they lived. After the establishment of the modern method of investigation (the inductive method) by Bacon and Descartes, they produced Benedict Spinoza (Holland and France, seventeenth century), one of the greatest of the world's thinkers; but he was a follower of Descartes, and gave up Judaism. So Moses Mendelssohn was a disciple of the German philosophers of his time. It is religion and not philosophy that Israel has given to the world.

5. Cabbala. — The mystical or gnostic teaching of the Jews is called Cabbala (the word means " tradition "), and those who study it Cabbalists. It is an attempt to explain the universe (including man) and its relation to God mystically. The Jews began this study early, but how they were led to it we don't know. No doubt it was once useful in inciting men to think about the problems of the soul; but it is too fanciful to produce permanently good results. The two great books of the Cabbala are the Yesira and the Sohar, written about the thirteenth century.

6. The Karaites. — It is interesting to observe that one small section of the Jews did not follow the Talmud, that is, the oral tradition, but confined themselves to the Scripture, whence they were called Karaites (from the Hebrew word *kara*, "scripture," or, "to read "). They are a small and uninfluential body, strict in life, but narrow in thought and culture. They are now found chiefly in Russia, Turkey, and Egypt.

7. Poetry. — We should expect to find that so active a people as the Jews had addicted themselves somewhat to poetry in the various lands of their dispersion. In fact, they have always followed the lead of their neighbors in this respect. In Alexandria they imitated the Greek poets (Lesson XXII.). At a later time they felt the stimulus of the Syrian Christians and the Moslem Arabs. When they settled in Europe, they wrote poetry in Spain, France, Italy, and Germany, which was based on models furnished them in these countries. And therefore, though there is a large mass of poetry written by Jews since the origination of the Talmud, there is, properly speaking, no Jewish poetry. As the Israelites spoke Arabic or Spanish or French or German or Italian, so they wrote Arabic, Spanish, French, German, or Italian poetry, though they may have used the Hebrew language. They have always kept up the study of their ancient tongue.

LITERATURE.

1. On Philo and Josephus: articles in cyclopedias. Mangay's English translation of Philo is published by Bohn. English translations of Josephus are easily accessible; of the Wars the best is Trail's.

2. On the Targums: there is a very good article in Smith's Bible Dictionary; English translations of Onkelos and Jonathan, by J. W. Etheridge, London.

3. On the Masora: articles in Herzog and Schenkel; books of Introduction.

4. On the commentators, philosophers, and cabbalists: Jost, "Geschichte des Judenthums;" Etheridge, "Introduction to Hebrew Literature."

5. On the poets: the above-mentioned; and Delitzsch's "Geschichte der Jüdischen Poesie."

QUESTIONS.

What is the relation of the Talmud to the Pentateuch? What may these two books be said to give? Before looking at the later literature, what two famous Jewish writers must be mentioned? What do they represent? When did Philo live? What did he do? What is the date of Josephus? The outline of his life? What did he write?

1. Why did the Jews have translations of their Scriptures? What version had they in Egypt? What are targums? Were they at first oral or written? Which is the earliest of the written targums? What new Greek version was produced at this time? Why was it written? What was the next targum after Onkelos? What targums followed? In what respect are they valuable?

2. What is the masora? Who are the Masorites? Can you mention the three things that they did? What text of the Old Testament do existing Hebrew manuscripts give? Can we learn from them certainly the text of Christ's time? What earlier authorities for this latter text have we? [The Greek and Aramaic versions, and the quotations in the New Testament.]

3. From whom did the Jews catch the grammatical spirit? Did they make many Hebrew grammars and dictionaries? Can you mention one famous grammarian? Of whom was he a contemporary? When did Christian Europe begin the study of Hebrew?

4. Have the Jews composed many commentaries on the Bible and the Talmud? Are these valuable? Who is the most famous Talmud commentator? What saying had the Jews about him? Have the Jews ever had any real philosophy of their own? What great Jewish thinker lived in the seventeenth century?

5. What is the Cabbala? Is it now useful? Was it formerly useful?

6. Who are the Karaites? Have they ever been influential? Where are some of them now found?

7. Have the Jews written much poetry since the time of the Talmud? Is it, properly speaking, Israelitish or Jewish poetry? Why not? Have they always kept up the study of Hebrew?

LESSON XXVIII.

OUTWARD HISTORY FROM THE FALL OF JERUSALEM.

1. Proselyting.—It is a noteworthy fact that, for several centuries about the beginning of our era, the religion of Israel made numerous converts among the pagan peoples. Judaism was not missionary, it was proselyting; which is equivalent to saying that it was a national and not a universal religion like Christianity: it did not make organized efforts to press its national faith on other peoples, but it required them, when they adopted it, to become Jews. It was anxious for the triumph of Judaism rather than of pure religion; this was the disposition that Jesus denounced (Matt. xxiii. 15). About the beginning of our era the old religions of the Greek, Roman, and Semitic world were in process of dissolution; the people had outgrown them, and ceased to find in them satisfaction for their religious needs. Judaism, with its lofty conception of God and its strict ethical code and its authoritativeness, proved attractive to many minds. There were thousands of proselytes all over the Roman empire, and in the outlying lands. These were of two classes: the proselytes of the gate conformed to Jewish customs except circumcision; the proselytes of righteousness were circumcised, and became members of the Jewish people; the former are called "devout men" in the English New Testament. The Jewish faith was everywhere influential. A wife of the Emperor Nero is said to have been a proselyte. The satirist Juvenal ridicules the power of Jewish teachers over the Roman women. The royal family of Adiabene (a country lying just east of the Tigris, near Nineveh) embraced Judaism; King Izates underwent circumcision, and his mother, Helena, enriched the temple with great gifts. This was in the time of the Emperor Claudius. There were Jewish tribes in Arabia, and not a few of the inhabitants adopted their faith. But these triumphs of the religion of Israel were destined to be short-lived. They served chiefly to prepare the way for Christianity and Islam. The national faith of Israel could not permanently pass the boundaries of the nation.

2. **History in Palestine.** — The outward history of the Jews after the destruction of Jerusalem has little general interest. It is the history not of a nation but of detached communities. In Palestine they were restless under the heavy yoke of the Romans, and in Trajan's time (A.D. 115) there were bloody uprisings by their brethren in Cyrene and Cyprus. The Romans resolved to root out the Israelitish religion, which they felt to be incompatible with the unity of the empire. Trajan caused the temple-mount to be ploughed up. His successor, Hadrian, built a Roman city on the site of Jerusalem, called it Aelia, after his family, and forbade Jews to enter it. This harshness drove the unhappy people to revolt. An adventurer, who went by the name of Bar-cochba (Son of a Star, in allusion to Num. xxiv. 17), proclaimed himself the Messiah, sent by God to deliver the nation from the Romans. He was acknowledged by the famous

rabbi Akiba; thousands of men flocked to his standard, and a fierce war ensued, speedily terminated by the defeat and death of the pretended Messiah and the execution of Akiba and thousands of his countrymen. The Jews were again crushed to the earth, and after this made no more attempts at independence in their own land. They continued for some time to have a religious organization, at the head of which was a Nasi, or Prince, whose religious authority was acknowledged by the whole Jewish world; but Palestine was no longer theirs. Some of them have lived on there ever since; a few thousands are now dwelling on the sacred soil, to which many go to die and be buried; but the body of the people have transferred themselves to other lands. Whether the nation will ever return to Palestine, it is impossible to say; it seems unlikely now.

3. In Babylonia. — The Babylonian Jews had formed a prosperous community ever since the Exile, surviving repeated changes of foreign dynasties, and pursuing legal studies with marked success. In this later time, as the Palestinians had their Nasi, so the Babylonians had their Resh Glutha, or Head of the Captivity, who exercised the functions of a civil and religious chief in his own district, and paid a partial and not always willing homage to his metropolitan brother in Palestine. There was considerable activity in the schools, resulting in elaboration of the ritual and ethical law, but there was no real advance in religion. The Babylonian Jews had their trials and sufferings, like their brethren in other parts of the world. The monarchs of the new Persian kingdom (the Sassanide, founded in the third century of our era) were zealous adherents of the Zoroastrian religion, and not unfrequently persecuted their Jewish subjects. In 651 A.D. the Sassanide kingdom was conquered by the Moslem Arabs, and the Jews remained undisturbed under the rule of their new masters. Apart from the oppression of local governors, indeed, their condition was bettered by this change of affairs. The Arabian Califs became patrons of science and art. Learned Jews were put into positions of trust, and Jewish thought was affected by Arabian science. So it continued till towards the middle of the eleventh century, when the

Jewish Babylonian Patriarchate (that is, the office of the Resh Glutha) ceased to exist, and the people were scattered. Many of them went to Egypt, Spain, and other countries, and those who remained were absorbed in the neighboring population.

4. In Europe. — Driven out of Asia the Jews began a new and vigorous life in Europe. They settled by thousands in Spain and the adjoining countries. They devoted themselves to learning and the accumulation of wealth. They became famous as bankers, physicians, and philosophers. Self-contained and persistent, they were equally necessary to the Moslem and the Christian princes of Spain in the long series of wars between these powers. The histories of the Middle Ages abound in curious narratives of Jewish energy and success. The Moslems favored and fostered them. Christian bigotry finally drove them from Spain (Ferdinand and Isabella). But they flourished in France, England, Italy, and Germany. They had innumerable synagogues, schools, and commercial houses. Often persecuted and plundered, hated and despised as enemies of Christianity, they grew steadily in numbers and power. As the Christian nations advanced in enlightenment, they saw the folly of their treatment of the Jews, and accorded them more and more privileges. At the present day their legal status is, with a few exceptions, the same as that of other people. Their social ostracism remains ; this is partly the fault of their intense self-assertion and lack of social culture, and partly the fault of Christian race-prejudice. Their religion has ceased to have any attraction for those who are not born Jews.

5. Messianic Expectations. — After Bar-cochba's failure the rabbis continued to discuss the Messianic question, but without notable result. The opinion sprang up that there would be two Messiahs, one a son of Joseph, who should suffer and perish, the other a son of David, who should be victorious and found a Jewish kingdom. But circumstances rarely permitted the scattered sons of Israel to make a serious attempt at establishing a nationality. One curious episode of this sort may be mentioned: a certain Shabbathai Zwi, born in Smyrna in 1641, raised the Messianic standard in Turkey. Thousands of Jews, including many learned men, acknowledged his pretensions and followed him. The East was filled with joy; Zwi set out to march to Jerusalem, and was everywhere received by his countrymen with royal honors. But the farce speedily ended. The pretender was summoned before the sultan, and there denied his Messianic claims, and embraced Islam. There was a similar attempt a few years ago in Yemen (Arabia), and the Orthodox Jews still look for a son of David who shall lead them back to their own land.

LITERATURE.

Etheridge's Introduction; Jost's Geschichte; various histories of the Moslems, of Spain, England, and other European countries; F. D. Mocatta, "The Jews of Spain and Portugal," London, 1877.

QUESTIONS.

1. Did Judaism make converts among the pagans? Was it a missionary religion? What is a proselyting spirit? What was true of the old religion at the beginning of our era? Why did Judaism prove attractive to many minds? What were the two classes of proselytes? What instances can you give of the spread of Jewish religious ideas? Were these triumphs permanent? For what did they serve?

2. Why has the later outward history of the Jews little general interest? What was the condition in Palestine? What did the Romans resolve to do? What did Trajan do?—Hadrian? What was the result? Can you describe the uprising under Bar-cochba? What organization did the Palestine Jews continue to have? Have they ever since possessed the land? Do some of them still dwell there? What of the nation's again returning thither?

3. What had been the condition of the Babylonian Jews since the Exile? What organization had they in later times? What was the result of the work of the schools? What was the condition of the Babylonian Jews under the Sassanide kingdom?—under the Moslems? How long did the Babylonian Patriarchate last? What then became of the people?

4. Whither did the Jews go from Asia? In what countries did they settle? To what did they devote themselves? Were they especially successful in Spain? Which power favored them? What drove them from Spain? When? Where did they flourish? What has been the result of the ad-

vancement of Christian nations in enlightenment? What is the present legal status of the Jews? What are the reasons of their social ostracism? Is their religion attractive to other peoples?

5. In later times what opinion concerning the Messiah sprang up? Could the Jews easily attempt to establish a nationality? Can you relate the episode of Shabbathai Zwi? For what do the Orthodox Jews still look?

LESSON XXIX.

THE REFORM.

1. Intellectual Isolation of the Jews. — The main reason why the Jews in Europe remained devoted to their religious traditions was their ignorance of the advancing culture of the world. In Spain, it is true, where they were liberally treated by the Moslems, they had learned something of Greek philosophy through Arabic translations. But in the succeeding centuries, under bigoted Christian governments, they were cut off by Christian prejudice from intercourse with the new world of thought. They were condemned to live in separate quarters in cities (like the Ghetto in Rome); they were denied access to the universities; they were treated in all respects as unclean, and it was thought a great kindness that they were barely tolerated. Thus they were shut up within themselves, and the breath of modern thought did not blow upon them.

2. Progress. — But the condition of things gradually improved. This separation between man and man, the result of barbarous ignorance and prejudice, could not exist in the face of growing enlightenment. Here and there were Israelites who came under the influence of wider spheres of thought, and broke through the trammels of their national tradition. Some of these became Christians, some rejected both Christianity and Judaism, and many, no doubt, remaining in the Israelitish community, became centres of more liberal thought in small circles. The eighteenth century brought with it an upheaval of old social, political, and religious ideas. In France this movement culminated in the Revolution, but it made itself felt all over Europe, and the Jews reaped benefit from it, especially in Prussia. Germany was destined to be the cradle of the Jewish emancipation, as it had been of the Christian two and a half centuries before. In 1750 Frederick the Great issued his famous edict defining the status of the Jews, and ordering their life. The effect of this decree was to bring the long-banished people back into relation with their fellows, and to subject them to the influence of the broader Christian thought. The result began to be seen immediately. Some of the Jews availed themselves of their new opportunities. Then naturally two parties arose, one favoring the adoption of new ideas, the other devoted to the maintenance of the old (and this was not the first time that such a state of things had existed in Israel). The party of progress increased slowly, but it lacked a leader. This lack was shortly supplied by the appearance of the remarkable man of whom we must now say a word.

3. Moses Mendelssohn. — The third Moses was destined to exert a hardly less controlling influence over his countrymen than his two great predecessors (see Lesson XXVII. 4). He appeared at the critical time when the Jews needed a directing mind to bring their national feeling and thought into harmony with the scientific and philosophical culture of the new Europe. To this work he devoted his whole life with rare single-mindedness, simplicity, and soundness of judgment. He was twenty-one years old when Frederick's edict was issued, and he lived up to the verge of the French Revolution (died, 1786); he was thus in the centre of the great German and European movement of enlightenment. He had been introduced, almost by accident, to the modern broader thought, of which he became an expounder to his countrymen. He worked his way into sympathy with the best and most active minds of the time; he was the friend of Lessing and Lavater. At the same time he remained an Israelite. His national feeling was strong; what he tried to do was to show his people that they might remain true Israelites, and yet accept what was valuable in the philosophical and religious thought of the time. He was not radical in feeling or action, but rather made it his aim to build on the existing foundation of Jewish thought. In order to provide biblical reading for his children he began a German translation of the Old Testament, with notes; and this translation, in which the utterances of the ancient inspired men of Israel were treated as fresh, living truth, and disengaged from the rabbinical mummy-cloths, proved of inestimable advantage to the people, by bringing them into contact with simple, earnest religious truth and life. It was in this way that he led them into a new path, and became the founder of the Reform. He was bitterly opposed by a portion of the rabbinical party, but he kept on his way undisturbed. He sowed seeds that were to bring forth fruit beyond what he himself thought of.

4. Progress since Mendelssohn. — The impulse given by Mendelssohn produced various tendencies in Jewish thought and effort, and gave rise to various problems. He himself, though opposed by some of the rabbis, had, through his conservatism, maintained friendly relations with the rabbinical party in general, and some of his friends and followers continued to pursue this course. Others were more inclined to break with rabbinism, and throw off everything distinctively Jewish. Others, again, attempted, but unsuccessfully, a union with the Christians. These different tendencies have continued to exist up to the present day. At the same time measures were taken to organize more perfectly the religious government by means of councils and rabbinical officers, and to simplify the services of the synagogue. These various lines of progress were carried on not only in Prussia, but also in France, Holland, and England. Everywhere there was movement; men were inquiring into the reasons of things, and trying to improve them. The result was a general progress in freedom of thought, great increase of scientific work, and marked simplification of the religious creed.

5. The Present Condition of the Reform. — The Reform to-day includes a majority of the Jews of Europe and America. These reject the authority of the tradition, and have thrown off many of the old religious rites and customs, retaining, however, circumcision. Their religion has assumed the general form of simple theism, but with many varieties of creed. Their public worship approaches in form and spirit that of the Christians. Their attitude towards Christianity is friendly; they revere Jesus of Nazareth as a great ethical and religious reformer. They enter warmly into the spirit of modern life, and are distinguished in most departments of scientific research. The social barriers which have hitherto separated them from the Gentiles are slowly disappearing. But in proportion as they move in this direction, they lose their distinctively Jewish character. Their God is not the Yahwe of the prophets, but the God of reason. Their national development is merged in the general current of the world's thought.

6. The Orthodox. — A respectable number of Jews still hold to the Talmud and the traditional law. These constitute the Rabbinical or Orthodox party. They are most numerous in Austria, but are found all over the world. They cannot be said, however, to reproduce exactly the traditionalists of the early centuries; except in some remote corners of Europe and Asia, they too have been touched by the modern spirit. The differences between them and the Reformed may be studied in the synagogues which are found in all our cities.

LITERATURE.

1. On the history of the Reform movement: the works of Jost and Herzfeld above mentioned; Barclay, "The Talmud;" Felix Adler, "Reformed Judaism," North American Review, vol. 125; Dr. Gottheil, "The Position of the Jews in America," North American Review, vols. 126, 127.

2. On the writings of Mendelssohn and others: Etheridge's Introduction.

3. On the social and religious life of the Jews: J. F. Schröder, "Satzungen und Gebräuche des Judenthums," Bremen, 1851.

QUESTIONS.

1. Why did the European Jews remain devoted to their tradition? What was the reason of their ignorance? What was their condition?

2. What improvement gradually came to pass? What happened to individual Israelites? What did the eighteenth century bring with it? Was this movement felt all over Europe? What country became the cradle of Jewish emancipation? What edict was issued by Frederick the Great? When? What was its effect? What two parties arose? What was lacking? Was the lack soon supplied?

3. At what critical time did Moses Mendelssohn appear? To what did he devote his life? At what time did he live? Of what did he become an expounder to his countrymen? Did he remain an Israelite? What did he try to do? Was his course radical? What translation did he undertake? What was its effect? With what did he bring his people into contact?

4. What was the result of the impulse given by Mendelssohn? What different directions did his followers take? What other measures were set on foot? Where? What was the result of all this?

5. What does the Reform now include? What do they reject? What form has their religion assumed? What of their public worship? — their attitude towards Christianity? — their relation to modern life? — their social position? What effect does this have on their distinctively Jewish character? What of their national development?

6. Who constitute the Orthodox party? What other name may be given them? Where are they found? Have they been affected by modern progress?

LESSON XXX.

CONCLUSION.

1. The Persistence of the Religion of Israel. — The history of the religion of Israel, which we have rapidly gone over, exhibits its remarkable tenacity of life. It has survived all the changes in the outward and inward condition of the people, and is to-day, four thousand years after the Hebrews entered Canaan, professed, revered, and followed by multitudes of their descendants. No other religion in the world has enjoyed so long a recorded life. This persistency is to be ascribed, in part, to its elevated conceptions of God and man, which gave it the advantage over its rivals; but in part, also, to the vigor of the Jewish race, which has maintained the separate existence of the people for so many centuries in the midst of strangers. These are the human agencies that God has employed to preserve this religion which has been so powerful a factor in the history of the human race.

2. Its Character and Growth. — The facts that have come to our knowledge make it probable that all the ancient or national religions originated in the same way, and grew according to the same laws. The differences between them are the differences between the peoples to whom they belonged. Up to a certain point in their development they are all alike, and then they begin to show their local peculiarities. Of the earliest stage in the growth of Israel's religion, the fetishistic, we know almost nothing; when we first find them in Canaan, they are polytheists, like their neighbors, that is, they had separated the Deity from the objects of nature, and regarded these last as symbols of the Godhead. Thus much of their religious career belongs to the general history of ancient religions. We are more interested in the succeeding development, which may be dated from the time of Samuel. In this we may note the two following stages: 1. There was the period of *conflict* between polytheism and monotheism, extending from Samuel to the Exile. It is described in the Old Testament as a struggle between Yahwe and the other gods. In this conflict there were two elements: the religious, that is, the recognition of the fact that there was no god but Yahwe, and the ethical, that is, the recognition of God's perfect holiness and his requirement of holiness from his servants. These two went hand in hand. Just this process went on in other nations, only it stopped at a certain point. Israel is distinguished from other ancient peoples by the fact that it pressed on till it reached the conception of the one holy God. We cannot tell exactly how it attained to this truth. We can see the general character of the historical progress: the basis was Israel's intense sentiment of nationality, and its deep-seated conviction that Yahwe, as its God, was above the other gods; from this, the deeper religious thinkers, seeing how all nations were bound together, were led to assert Yahwe's kingship over all the world, and then there was no need of any other god; at the same time, the highest ethical conceptions of the best men were identified with the Deity, as was the case in other nations also, only with greater precision and completeness in Israel; the prophets declared that Yahwe punished the sins of his own people as well as of other nations; finally, the Exile sifted Israel, and placed the religious development in the hands of the most advanced religious thinkers; the more superficial element was set aside, and the new nation was monotheistic. 2. There was the period of religious *law*, that is, the effort to order man's life in accordance with the will of God. Having reached the idea of a holy God, the next aim of Israel was to secure holiness of life. This they tried to secure by fixed rules, which they kept on increasing till these became burdensome and injurious. It was a noble attempt at the perfecting of life, but it was not successful. It established the idea of man's obligation to be holy, but it failed to show him the way. It was at this point that Jesus of Nazareth came forward, and taught that holiness was reached, not by rules, but by the inward disposition of love to God. But Israel was too firmly convinced of the rightness of its own method to listen to him. It continued, and has continued to this day, to make law its life, only demonstrating more and more fully the insufficiency of any set of rules for the perfecting of man's life. The mission of the religion of Israel was finished when the higher teaching of Jesus came. Its existence since that time has been only the semblance of life; and, as we have seen, the Jews have had to abandon it just in proportion as they have come under the influence of modern thought.

3. Its Legacy to us. — It is worth while for us to remember how closely our religious life is connected with that of Israel. The Bible is our store-house of religious thought and feeling, and the Bible, Old Testament and New Testament, is Israelitish. In the prophets and psalmists we have the record of the national religious life of the ancient Israel; in the evangelists and apostles we have the later Jewish ideas transformed by faith in Jesus as the Christ of God. Our fundamental religious ideas, *God, sin, redemption,* are of Israel. These, together with the belief in the *future life* (which, though not prominent in the Old Testament, was part of the faith of the later Judaism), Christianity inherited from the religion of Israel. To trace our religious pedigree, therefore, we have to go back to the prophets and the Law. We have seen how a pure monotheistic basis for religion was reached in ancient Israel. Along with this grew the conception of sin, first as an offence against the sovereignty of the divine king of Israel, and then as an offence against his law; out of which came the deeper conception of it as a violation of man's conscience, regarded as the image and expounder of the perfect holiness of God. Israel held sin to involve accountability to God, but it did not leave the sinner hopeless, — it trusted in the mercy of God, which provided redemption and salvation for his servants who repent and turn to him. Christianity may be called the development of the pure spiritual elements of the faith of Israel. The latter is not dead, but lives in the faith of the Christian world.

LITERATURE.

On the history of doctrine: Schultz, "Alttestamentliche Theologie," Frankfurt a. Main, 1878; Oehler, "Theology of the Old Testament" (English translation).

QUESTIONS.

1. What is to be said of the persistence of the religion of Israel? How is it to be explained?

2. What is true of the early stages of all national religions? When does the religious career of Israel become interesting? What two periods may be noted? Can you describe the period of conflict? — the period of law?

3. What book have we received from Israel? What fundamental religious ideas? What was Israel's conception of sin and redemption? In what does the faith of Israel still live?

INDEX.

Aaron, 20, 30.
Abarbanel, 135.
Aben Ezra, 135.
Abimelech, 30.
Abraham, 15, 16.
Adar, month, 95.
Adiabene, 139.
Aelia, city, 139.
Ahab, 43, 44, 47.
Ahasuerus, 95.
Ahaz, 56, 58, 62.
Ahijah, the prophet, 42.
Akiba, rabbi, 140.
Alexander Jannæus, 101, 123.
Alexander the Great, 86, 94.
Alexandria, 90, 105, 111, 136.
Allegory, 106.
Alliances, foreign, 61.
Amalekites, 10, 34.
Ammonites, 10, 37, 54, 69, 71, 75.
Amon, king, 66.
Angels, 86, 109, 110.
Antipater, 101, 123.
Aphorisms, 104.
Apocalypse, 108.
Apocrypha, the, 116.
Apologues, religious, 95.
Apothegms, 96.
Aquila, Greek version of, 134.
Arabs, 9, 69.
Aramæans, 9.
Aramaic language, 126, 133.
Aristobulus, king, 101, 123.
Aristotle, 136.
Ark, the, 21, 30, 32, 37, 38.
Artaxerxes Longimanus, 86, 90.
Ashe, rabbi, 130.
Asher, the deity, 12.
Ashera, the goddess, 44, 45, 59, 66.
Ashtaroth, the, 47.
Ashtoreth, 66.
Asiatic nations, sacred books of, 113.
Assyrian monuments, 40.
Assyrians, 9, 43, 49, 50, 53, 55, 56, 57, 58, 64, 69.
Athaliah, 45, 49, 50.
Avilmarduk (Evil-Merodach), king, 70.
Baal, 43, 44, 47, 66, 100.
Baasha, king, 43.
Babylon, 40, 58, 81, 82, 84, 103.
Babylonia, 86
Babylonians, 61, 69, 70, 76, 79, 80, 81, 109.
Bar-cochba, 139.
Baruch, 72.
Baruch, book of, 111.
Baths, public, 124.
Bedawin, 14.
Beersheba, 50.
Bethel, 43, 54.
Bethlehem, 36.
Bigotry, Christian, 141.
Blessings and curses, 67.
Book, people of the, 90.
Books, Greek order of, 116.
Books, Hebrew order of, 116.
Books, lost, 114.
Books, sacred, 90, 99, 114, 118, 120.
Cæsar, 101, 123.
Calendar, Jewish, 122.
Canaanites, 9, 10, 28.
Canon, the, 105.
Canon, the first, 114.
Canon, the second, 115.
Canon, the third, 116.
Canon, discussions of the, 116.
Captives in Babylon, 79, 84.
Captivity, Assyrian, 57, 74.
Captivity, head of the, 140.
Caucasian race, 9.
Chaldeans, 69, 70, 71, 81, 111.
Chants, Gregorian, 104.
Chemosh, 23, 66.
Christ, the, 62, 64, 70, 72, 75, 77, 82, 87, 89, 106, 110, 114, 122, 123, 124, 126, 131, 134, 138, 146, 149, 150.
Church, 76, 85, 95, 119.

INDEX.

Circumcision, 16.
Claudius, emperor, 139.
Clement of Alexandria, 111.
Code, religious, 20, 25, 52, 67, 76, 80.
Code, ritual, 119, 120.
Commerce, Hebrew, 38.
Conflict, period of religious, 143.
Council (Sanhedrin), 121.
Covenant, the new, 114.
Covenant, the old, 114.
Crassus, 123.
Creation, story of, 91.
Cyprus, 139.
Cyrene, 139.
Cyrus, 40, 75, 81, 84.
Dagon, 24.
Damascus, 58.
Dan, city, 43, 54.
Darius Hystaspis, 85.
David as poet, 38, 104.
David Kimchi, 135.
Davidic king, prosperity under, 63, 80.
Deborah, 29.
Decalogue, two versions of, 25.
Dedication, feast of, 100.
Deities, foreign, 24, 30, 33, 39, 44, 45, 47, 55, 59, 65, 66.
Deuteronomy, book of, 19, 67, 91.
Domesday-book, the Israelitish, 29.
Ecclesiastes, 106.
Ecclesiasticus, 105.
Edomites, 10, 37, 54, 77, 80, 101.
Egypt, 14, 72, 84, 86, 99.
Egyptians, 13, 45, 58, 64, 70.
Eighth century B.C., the, 51.
Elders of tribes, 10.
Elegy on Saul and Jonathan, 38.
Elias Levita, 135.
Elihu, 97.
Elohim-narrative, 92.
Elyon, 12.
Embassy to Rome, Jewish, 101.
Ephod, 30.
Ephraim, tribe of, 27, 29, 42.
Essenes, the, 101.
Esther, additions to, 95.
Ethiopian, 58.
Eusebius, 111.
Exodus, book of, 19, 91.
Exodus, date of the, 18.
Exodus, origin of, 91.
Ezekiel, tragic poet, 111.
Ezra, 86, 87, 90, 93, 114, 115, 121.

Ezra, third book of, 111.
Fasts, 85.
Ferdinand and Isabella, 141.
Festivals, 21, 90.
Fetishism, 11, 148.
Flood, narrative of the, 92.
Foreigners in Palestine, 86.
Fortune-tellers, 33.
Frederick the Great, edict of, 144.
Future life (Egyptian), 21.
Future life (Hebrew), 21, 96, 105, 106, 150.
Gad, deity, 12.
Galilee, 125, 126.
Gamaliel, 121.
Games, Greek, 100.
Gath, 37.
Gemara, language of the, 130.
Genesis i.–xi., 77.
Genesis, origin of, 91.
Genesis-stories, 15.
Gerizim, mount, 86, 101.
Ghetto, the, 143.
Gideon, 30.
God, kingdom of, 109.
Goliath, 36, 104.
Greek language, 86, 126.
Greeks, 9, 61, 86, 109.
Gymnasiums, 100.
Hadrian, emperor, 139.
Haggada, 131.
Hagiographa, the, 116.
Hagiographa, targums of, 134.
Halacha, 131.
Hamites, 9.
Hasidim, the, 100.
Hebrew, study of, 135, 137.
Hebrews, origin of. 10.
Helena, queen, 139.
Heliopolis, 86.
Hellenizers, 100.
Hercules, 30.
Herod the Great, 101, 123.
Herodians, the, 124.
Hexateuch, the, 115.
Hezekiah, annals of, 62.
Hezekiah, king, 58, 104.
Hieroglyphic writing, 14.
High places, 50.
High priest, 32, 121, 125.
Hilkiah, priest, 68.
Hillel, 121, 123.
Hillel, saying of, 121.
Histories, 52.

INDEX.

Hittites, 28.
Hoshea, king, 57.
Host of heaven, 11, 66.
Idolatry, 11, 23, 24, 30, 39, 43, 45, 47, 50, 54, 59, 63, 65, 66, 72, 75, 76, 82, 84, 110.
Idumeans, 101.
Indo-Europeans, 9.
Isaiah, disciples of, 66.
Isaiah xl.-lxvi., 81, 116.
Isaiah liii , 76, 82.
Islam, 139.
Itinerary, the, 27.
Izates, king, 139.
Jacob, 15, 54.
Jael, 29.
Jamnia, 129.
Jehoahaz, king, 70.
Jehoiachin, 70, 75, 79.
Jehoiada, 49.
Jehoiakim, king, 70, 72, 75.
Jehoshaphat, 45.
Jehuda, rabbi, 129.
Jephthah, 30.
Jeremiah, epistle of, 111.
Jeroboam II., 49, 95.
Jerusalem, capture of, 125.
Jerusalem, centre of worship, 65.
Jerusalem, destruction of, 125, 129.
Jesus, father of Sirach, 105.
Jesus, son of Sirach, 105.
Jethro, 19.
Jews, the orthodox, 142.
Jews, ostracism of, 141, 143.
Jews in Arabia, 139.
Jews in Austria, 146.
Jews in Babylonia, 79, 90, 93, 115, 126.
Jews in Egypt, 86.
Jews in England, 145.
Jews in France, 145.
Jews in Holland, 145.
Jews in Prussia, 144, 145.
Jews in Russia, 136.
Jezebel, 44.
Jezreel, 49.
Joab, 37.
John Hyrcanus I., 101.
John Hyrcanus II., 101, 123.
Jonathan, son of Saul, 38.
Jonathan, targum of, 134.
Jonathan, the Hasmonean, 100.
Joseph, 15.
Josephus, Flavius, 101, 125, 132.

Josiah, king, 68, 70, 71, 111.
Judah, tribe of, 27, 29, 37, 42.
Judaism, 89, 127, 128.
Judas Maccabæus, 100, 111.
Jude, book of, 110.
Judeans, 79, 99.
Judith, book of, 112.
Jupiter, altar of, 99.
Kebar, canal, 79.
Ketubim, the, 116.
Koran, the, 114.
Kushite, 58.
Law books, 52, 67, 91.
Law, students of, 119.
Law, period of religious, 149.
Laws, ceremonial, 91.
Laws, codification of, 122.
Laws of early tribes, 10, 11.
Lawyers, 115, 120.
Legalists, 95.
Letters, Phœnician, 126.
Leontopolis, 86.
Levites, 30, 44, 84, 91, 104.
Leviticus, book of, 19, 59, 91.
Leviticus, origin of, 91.
Locusts, plague of, 87.
Luther, 65, 90, 135.
Maccabees, the, 84.
Maccabees, first book of, 111.
Maccabees, second book of, 111.
Maimonides, 135.
Magic, 66.
Man, Son of, 110.
Manasseh, king, 66, 68.
Manhood, religious, 75.
Manuscripts, 119, 120, 135.
Mardochæus, 95.
Mariamne, 124.
Masbal, 39.
Mattathias, 100.
Medes, 69, 81, 84, 109.
Megiddo, battle of, 70.
Mendelssohn, Moses, 136.
Mendelssohn, translation of Old Testament, 145.
Menephtah, king, 17.
Mesopotamia, 9, 79.
Messiah, ben-Joseph, 141.
Messiah, the, 61, 110, 127, 139.
Micaiah, the prophet, 53.
Midrash, the, 131.
Milcom, 66.
Miriam, 20.

154 INDEX.

Mishna, language of the, 130.
Mishna, orders of the, 129.
Moabites, 10, 37, 54, 69, 71, 73, 75.
Modin, city, 100.
Monotheism, 24, 25, 37, 55, 75, 76, 119, 148.
Moon, worship of the, 11, 66.
Mordecai, 95.
Moriah, mount, 30.
Moslems, the, 58, 135, 136, 140, 141.
Most High, saints of the, 110.
Music, 33, 94, 103, 104.
Nadab, king, 43.
Names, plays on, 62.
Nasi (prince), 140.
Nebuchadnezzar, 57, 70, 74, 109, 130.
Necromancers, 34.
Nehemiah, 86, 115.
Nehushtan, 59.
Nero, 139.
Nineveh, 71, 95, 112, 139.
Numbers, book of, 19, 91.
Offerings, 67, 71, 76.
Onias, high-priest, 111.
Onkelos, targum of, 133.
Party, national, 100, 101.
Patriarchate, Babylonian, 141.
Patriarchs, the, 52.
Paul, the apostle, 54, 71, 121.
Pekah, king, 56.
Pentateuch, date of, 91.
Pentateuch, division of, 115
Pentateuch, meaning of, 90.
Pentateuch, Samaritan, 86.
Pentateuch, targums on, 134.
Period, scribal, 119.
Period, Greek, 105.
Persians, 9, 61, 81, 84, 85, 86, 87, 109.
Pharisees, the, 101, 120, 125.
Philistines, 10, 32, 58, 60, 71, 75.
Philo, 132.
Philosophy, 52, 96, 104, 106, 111.
Phocylides, 111.
Phœnicians, 9, 37, 54.
Pilate, Pontius, 124.
Pirke Aboth, 130.
Poems, 52.
Pompey, 101, 123.
Preachers, 60.
Priests, list of, 94.
Priests, power of, 89.
Priestly period, 83.
Princes of Judah, 72.

Prophecy, periods of, 61.
Prophetic discourses, 53.
Prophetesses, 110.
Prophets, former, 115.
Prophets, latter, 115.
Prophets, number of, 52.
Prophets, order of, 33.
Proverbs, 33, 96.
Psalm on Goliath, 104.
Psalms, five books of, 104.
Psalms, titles of, 104.
Psalter of Solomon, 104.
Purim, feast of, 95.
Rabbis, 122, 128.
Rameses II., 17.
Rameses, city, 16.
Ramoth Gilead, 49.
Rashi, 135.
Rechabites, the, 48.
Redemption, 150.
Reform, ancient, 48, 59, 65, 68, 89, 90, 121.
Religion, the Greek, 99, 138.
Religion, the Roman, 138.
Responsibility, personal, 80.
Restoration, the, 93, 94.
Resurrection, 87, 110.
Revelation, 108.
Revolution, French, 144.
Romances, historical, 112.
Romans, the, 9, 61, 99, 121, 123, 124, 125, 139.
Ruth, book of, 77.
Sabak (So), king, 57.
Sabbath, the, 21, 90, 120.
Sacrifice, human, 25, 31, 59, 66.
Sacrifices, 12, 67, 71, 76, 81, 89.
Sadducees, the, 101.
Sages, 38, 52, 67, 96, 97, 104, 106.
Samaria, city, 43.
Samaria, province, 57.
Samaritans, 57, 86, 117.
Samson, 30.
Sanctuary at Dan, 30, 43.
Sanhedrin, the, 116.
Sargon, king, 57.
Sassanide kingdom, 140.
Satan, 97.
Schools of prophecy, 53.
Schools, Rabbinical, 129.
Seers, 33, 109.
Seir, nation, 80.
Sennacherib, king, 58, 63.
Septuagint, 72, 86, 95, 115, 134.

Sermons, 53.
Serpent, bronze, 59.
Seventy years, the, 75.
Shabbathai Zwi, 141.
Shaddai, 12, 16, 24.
Shalmaneser IV., 49, 57.
Shammai, 121.
Sheol, 54, 55, 106.
Shiloh, 32, 33.
Shows, theatrical, 124.
Shrines, local, 59, 65, 67.
Simeon, tribe of, 42.
Simon, the Hasmonean, 100.
Sinai, 20, 27.
Sirbonian lake, the, 27.
Sohar, the, 136.
Spinoza, Benedict, 136.
Spontaneousness, prophetic, 114.
Stars, worship of, 11, 66.
Study, legal, 90.
Sumerian-Accadians, 22.
Sun, worship of, 11, 66.
Swine's flesh, 99.
Synagogue, the Great, 121.
Synagogues, 87, 120, 146.
Syria, 86, 99.
Syria, Greek kingdom of, 99, 100, 109.
Syriac language, 126.
Syrians, 9, 43, 49, 53, 56, 100.
Tabernacle, the, 30.
Tabernacles, feast of, 43.
Talmud, 126, 129.
Targums, the, 133.
Taxes, 42.
Tekoa, 53.
Tel-Abib, 79.
Temple of Herod, the, 124.
Temple, ritual of, 94.
Temple, the second, 85, 94.
Ten tribes, the, 42, 58, 74.
Teraphim, 24.
Testament, the New, 37, 72, 110, 114, 126, 131.
Testament, the Old, 114, 128.
Text, Masoretic, 134.

The Law and the Prophets, 116.
Tiberias, 129.
Tiglathpileser II., 56.
Tirhakah, king, 58.
Titus, 125.
Tobit, book of, 112.
Tora, 26, 90, 115, 128, 132.
Trade by barter, 11.
Traditions, 52, 91, 121, 122, 145.
Trajan, 139.
Tribe princes, 28.
Universities, Jews excluded from the, 143.
Urijah, priest, 59.
Urim and Thummim, 21.
Uzziah, 50.
Visions, 85, 109, 111.
Vowel-signs, 134.
Well-song, 52.
Wisdom personified, 105.
Wives, foreign, 90.
Wizards, 34.
Women, guild of, 32.
Women in Temple choir, 104.
Words counted, 134.
Worship of heavenly bodies, 11.
Writings, anonymous, 116.
Writings, the, 116.
Xerxes, 95.
Yahwe-narrative, 92.
Yahwe our Righteousness, 72.
Yahwe, pronunciation of, 23.
Yahwe, servant of, 81.
Yahwists, 33, 42, 44, 66.
Yemen, 142.
Yesira, 136.
Zachariah, king, 48.
Zealots, the, 125.
Zechariah ix.-xiv., 116.
Zedekiah, king, 70, 72.
Zedekiah, prophet, 53.
Zerubbabel, 84.
Zeus, altar of, 99.
Zion, 37, 62.
Zoroastrian religion, 140.

www.ingramcontent.com/pod-product-compliance
Lightning Source LLC
Chambersburg PA
CBHW020301170426
43202CB00008B/449